NOT FROM HERE:
the Song of America

Leah Lax

NOT FROM HERE:
the Song of America

Pegasus

PEGASUS PAPERBACK

© Copyright 2024
Leah Lax

The right of Leah Lax to be identified as author of
this work has been asserted by her in accordance with the
Copyright, Designs and Patents Act 1988

A CIP catalogue record for this title is
available from the British Library

ISBN-978 1 80468 017 9

*Pegasus is an imprint of
Pegasus Elliot MacKenzie Publishers Ltd.*
www.pegasuspublishers.com

First Published in 2024

**Pegasus
Sheraton House Castle Park
Cambridge CB3 0AX England**

Printed & Bound in Great Britain

This book is a tribute to the great Svetlana Alexeivich, and to our epic, fragile freedom.

With gratitude to Houston Endowment, the Brown Foundation, the Nathan Cummings Foundation, and Inprint, for their vision and their trust.

We bear each other, hoping to breathe in each other's freedom.

LAURENT BERLAND

It was as if he stood me squarely before the world, removed the blindfold, and ordered me to open my eyes.

CAROLYN FORCHÉ

Contents

Part One

The Curtain Rises

Not From Here began as an opera. Like a life still lived, its songs — its stories — are unfinished, as is mine. As is my country's. Each was given me as an offering, a shared rush to freedom. *Come closer*, these stories whisper. *Let me tell you how I did it, and you will know what we have a little bit more.* Every account reaches again and again for the fabled American Dream. It is a dream. "Not one of us was here when this house was built," Isabel Wilkerson wrote. We are heirs to its fissures, its cracks spreading beneath the surface.

I was born a grandchild of refugees, but my family never told me our stories; my grandparents' experiences in coming to the United States were intentionally buried in favor of their American Dream. All through my childhood, I wondered, *Who are we?*

What are we without our stories? Sometimes we write new ones in the void. As a teen when I found the Jewish ultra-Orthodox, I thought I had found the lost stories of my people. I left the girlfriend with whom I was in love and lived among them, largely apart from mainstream society, for thirty closeted years. Then, I lost my faith. I faced my secret desires. I left.

I became an immigrant in my own country, and I was blindsided with the acute desire of an outsider. Online cacophony was overwhelming. When out in public, I darted glances at the varied welter of humanity and found no answers. Mornings, the questions were waiting in the mirror: *Am I of this place? If so, who are we?* "We are all migrants through time," Mohsin Hamid wrote. It seemed he wrote that for me.

I finished graduate school, taught a few classes, and continued to hover on the edge like a stranger who wouldn't go home. Then I was asked to write an opera.

They wanted it based on immigrant stories of my immigrant city, but to write those voices, I had to know my city and speak its language. I went downtown to tell the opera director he was making a mistake, but then I was in Anthony Freud's crowded office sitting on the edge of a small white sofa, behind him, shelves with opera books, music books, and elegant items tastefully arranged. I knew I wanted this. I cleared my throat, pictured my refugee grandparents, and thought, *This is a whole nation of immigrant families; we are a nation of immigrants.*

It seemed in that moment that an underground train had always run beneath my family wafting its smoke and darkness long after their journey to this country was forgotten. *Was that it?* I thought. *The transition, the losses, never leave? Are we as a nation haunted by memories we don't know we have? The rumblings must be everywhere.*

Freud was talking, saying the new work should reflect the audience in all its colors and stories, that audience and singers would become facing mirrors in a mutually defining dance. There was his inquisitive face, his keen gaze. I will never know why he offered me this commission.

"It was said in those days that the passage was both like dying and like being born," Mohsin Hamid wrote. He meant the immigrant passage. He envisioned that passage a portal of darkness, then an emergence into light, into a fractured world.

I began to search my city for people willing to tell their stories, and I began to listen.

About a month into the project, I took a break and went into a nail salon run by a group of Vietnamese women. With the fingertips of my hand in a dish of warm soapy water, I asked the stylist holding my other hand for her story. I asked with the sincerity one might use to address an intimate, someone holding your hand. "Tell me, where are you from?" I said, *sotto voce*. "How did you come here?"

I imagined myself her friend asking uncomplicated questions, the answers to which I had a benign right to know. I couldn't hear my own subtext: *Of course, you're not from here, and I am.*

"I just like stories," I added, and couldn't hear this as trivializing her experiences. Then, as if offering enticement — proof of the great value of what I was doing — I told the woman that the mayor of Houston was interested in the project, in her story.

I think now with a sigh of how suspicious, how careful people in communist Vietnam had to become about interrogations by strangers after the war. To tell that woman that a government official was interested in her testimony! I didn't yet know about the millions of people the communist victors sent to prison camps for the most arbitrary of reasons; didn't imagine the woman holding my hand could have endured something like an armed official striding unannounced into her home who might, for example, count rice bowls in her cabinet and then arrest them all. 'There are five bowls here and only four people are registered to live in this house. Who are you hiding??'

The woman flinched at my question, a quick clench of my hand, and muttered something to the stylist at the next station. Chatter in Vietnamese, loud and agitated, exploded in the shop. They could not get me out of there fast enough.

Intimations of a secret past. I had found the rumblings. They were not so underground.

The one hundred twenty-three people who spoke to me that year were my teachers; they taught me America. They had come from around the world, had left their homes both voluntarily and involuntarily, fleeing war (wars my country had fed or caused or drove) or they fled persecution, or gangs, or poverty. They came for an education, or for a job, or marriage, or to join their family, or seeking safe haven. Every one of them came to the United States to start over.

We met in diners and restaurants, in coffeehouses, office buildings, corner stores, and auto shops, in used cars, school lobbies, parking lots, sparsely furnished apartments, and opulent suburban homes. I listened to men, women, and children. With each, I said, "Please begin with *I was born...*" I knew I was looking for far more information than I needed for an opera libretto, but It seemed I needed to know, why choose a life of uncertainty and sweeping change? Why leave your home to rebuild without a foundation?

They began slowly, even hesitantly, then sped up as if compelled, and could talk for hours. The accounts could be disjointed, or halting, the speaker exuberant, or determined, grieving, or damaged, triumphant, or angry, or starry-eyed, their English careful, or creative, educated, or nonexistent. As stories unfolded, old joys and traumas bloomed before us. Many had never told anyone before. The men tended to cry.

I had found the American Dream very much alive, and it spoke with an accent. Perhaps it always has. I had thought that old myth badly tarnished, but from my Hasidic past, I knew how a myth can offer timeless hope one may need to live. I gave that dream credit for being no less than such a myth.

With every speaker, I felt a keen affinity that I didn't understand. I thought, *But I was born here.* Now I know that I had been hoping to follow them more surely into America. Instead, I uncovered my country constantly rebuilding itself, found its great beating heart.

The Refuge, by Houston Grand Opera, debuted in November of 2007. In a nod to the treks so many endured, the performers sang barefoot. "Our stories are your stories," they sang. "Now, we are here."

Houston Grand Opera reprised the work the following spring at Miller Outdoor Theater in Houston's Hermann Park, at the center of the city. The Miller is an old bandshell that fronts a great grassy hill, sporting enormously tall amplifiers. I walked the hill that night, crowded with groups on blankets sharing food and drink and chattering in dozens of languages, including English, thousands of people from here and not from here but here *now*, children darting and laughing, and felt, finally, that I had come home.

Nine years later, January 2016

A Twitter feed pinged through my city. Immigration and Customs Enforcement had set up checkpoints at key intersections. There were arrests. "Stay home," people tweeted. "Stay away."

I paced the floor in my little rented duplex scrolling for news. Houston had a longstanding, unspoken policy of no immigration raids or profiling. I pictured a woman I had met for the opera project, short-haired and heavyset. She came to Texas as a migrant worker picking crops in the Rio Grande valley and sleeping outdoors, then made her way on foot hundreds of miles to Houston, where she obtained residency, then citizenship, and raised educated, productive children. "You know how one friend might give you dinner, but the next one is a better friend because he lets you go to the refrigerator yourself?" she said. "Houston is that kind of friend." When she said that, I heard, *The US is that kind of friend.*

The following year, deportations in my county went up two hundred percent.

2018

The online map was marked with red X's, each X a protest march of people expressing outrage about children being snatched from their parents by US patrol at our southern border. The screen was covered in red X's. My country was on fire. Another search, and another map indicated a rash of buildings in a five-mile radius around my home. I got in the car and went to one of them, on the border of Houston's enormous medical center.

The place loomed inscrutable, stripped of all signage, windows covered and blackened. Inside were over a thousand adults and hundreds of children who had come in pursuit of a dream. I got out and stood on the curb squinting in the Texas sun as cars zoomed by in this nation of immigrants.

Then the online map disappeared.

To the reader:

I edited out the ums and repetitions and "corrected" the grammar in these accounts with real regret, because doing so altered the rhythm of their music. I smoothed partial sentences and reset stories in the past tense that had been spoken all in the present as if the events were just then unfolding before them.

Theirs was a language that sang with the determination of survivors. Often, the speaker had learned English at work or on the streets, adopted phrases from television and street signs. I teared up as I worked to create a more familiar path for you to travel. I felt I was erasing their songs.

If you will, try to imagine these stories each in its own unique rhythm and music. Imagine a face with each account, each its own shape and shade. Maybe you will hear your own music as well, and your family's, in harmony or in beautiful dissonance to your own, and that will flesh out for you the 'we' of our country a little bit more.

Before you are some of America's most operatic of voices. Together, we make the music.

Part Two

We Fled Danger:
The Aftermath of War

Scene One

Luisa, *El Salvador*

It was 1986. My son Leib was seven, Libby was five, Yossie, three, Avrami was a toddler, and I was heavily pregnant. I moved as if through water from kitchen to playroom to the yard where the children played, where Gloria — fellow laundress, nanny, seamstress, cook, and my Spanish professor — watched, sort of. She was really watching a flock of birds in the ailing old elm. I dragged over a plastic chair. "Que estas mirando?" I said. *What are you looking at?*

She was patient with my limited Spanish. "In my country, there are no birds," she said, enunciating to help me understand.

"No birds? Really? How is that possible?"

Gloria was from El Salvador, where civil war had raged longer than I knew, in part because I paid little attention to the world and its news. She had run from that war, had once told me that the sound of gunfire had shaken her sanity. Even when she said that I didn't ask questions.

"Guns," she said. "There are no birds in my country because of gunfire. And people shoot them for food."

Sparrows as food…

"Not one?"

"I didn't see any for years, until I came here."

I nodded for a sympathetic moment, but Gloria's presence always threatened to breech the wall of the religious bubble in which we lived with things like guns and war and no more birds. I said nothing more. Instead, I turned to the children as if to reassure them of paradise.

Nineteen years later

It was one of those Houston spring mornings I loved, when warm sun couples with a cool wind. The city's signature azaleas were bursting everywhere in pinks and yellows and whites. I pulled into the circular drive of a stately brick home that sat like a crown on a hill in a neighborhood of manicured gardens, oil money, and velvet silence. I parked, rolled down a window, and settled to wait for the translator. A scent of roses was in the air.

Inside that house was the woman I had come to meet, who daily scrubbed already gleaming parquet floors, deodorized perfectly clean porcelain toilets, and dusted shining countertops. Millions like her and like Gloria were crossing our border with

Mexico every year despite patrols and walls, fleeing impossible circumstances.

Anthony Freud had heard of this woman from a Houston friend who, like him, was also from the UK. I imagined the conversation over afternoon tea. "Oh yes," the friend says, "Houston is quite different from England. Why, I hired a housekeeper, and as we speak, her son is coming to Houston in the trunk of someone's car!" Freud reaches for a biscuit and the endless sweep of humanity across our borders steps out of the shadows. He hears the music, fresh and alive.

The woman was small in stature, with a sturdy build and long, wavy hair. She said little at the door, simply indicated with a turn on her heels that we were to follow her into an elegant dining room, then gestured for us to sit at a carved maple table in chairs of rich brocade. Nearby was a marble-topped breakfront and on it, a crystal vase filled with a burst of yellow sunflowers. Only at our urging she took a seat as well, next to the translator, darting repeated glances at the door.

I made a short introduction and presented the release form, which she quickly signed. I felt I had done my homework, but as I clipped a microphone to her collar and switched on the recorder, I couldn't see the ghosts of El Salvador that had followed this woman and two million like her into my country, hovering over us all that day.

A glance at my notes: She was twenty-seven years old and had two boys, aged nine and eleven. She had immigration issues.

I had a vague idea that the opera company might help her find legal help, and that was all.

El Salvador is in Central America, which is an isthmus connecting two continents. East to west, El Salvador is sixty miles wide. It is a hundred sixty miles long. The country is smaller than Massachusetts and bordered by much larger Guatemala and Honduras, with a long Pacific coastline.

Officially it was American concern over Russian communist influence since Salvadoran rebels called themselves Marxists, but the real reason for the United States' involvement in El Salvador's long civil war was always there like an undercurrent — the drive to protect American corporate dollars in coffee production. That concern drove the Carter and Reagan administrations to fuel El Salvador's twelve-year war. The US paid billions to shore up the murderous Salvadoran regime against the rebels. The Salvadoran government used the money to fund roving military squads that gunned down tens of thousands of landless *campesinos*, that is, peasant farmers, usually unarmed. They could kill hundreds in a day, some in their homes, among them thousands of women and children. American involvement in the Salvadoran civil war was murder for hire. It was also a blood-soaked exercise in futility.

The rebel army professed to represent the landless *campesinos,* the ninety per cent of the country who wanted their land back. The campesinos were so named because they lived as if camping out in makeshift homes of mud and wattle, twigs, cardboard, tin, strips of cloth, stuff that could wash away in a rain shower. They often lived on or near land their families had lost to American interests back when US corporations first partnered with a few local coffee growers to consolidate production and push everyone else off the land.

El Salvador was the war we in the US weren't told we lost.

The woman we had come to meet was born in the capital of El Salvador as the long civil war ended. As she learned to walk, victorious rebels formed a political party. Government paramilitary units that once prowled the highways shut down. As she grew, campesinos gave up on regaining family land and moved to the cities. Elections were held; public schools opened; running water and electricity came to households, and now there was medical care. She was as a city girl. Yet, of this I felt sure: she grew up surrounded by families who still bore their wounds. I do not know how many dared to hope.

She began in a tremulous voice and gave only her first name, then cautioned me not to reveal even that. "I'll call you 'Luisa,'" I said. I would remember the sound of her voice even in my dreams.

"I was born in El Salvador in Via del Rosario — that's part of San Miguel."

San Miguel is the capital, a city of half a million in eastern El Salvador.

She seemed nervous. "My husband doesn't know my story. I've always been afraid to tell anyone," she said. Luisa took a breath. "We... we were four kids. I'm the youngest and the only girl. I was fourteen."

Fourteen, I thought. *School, girlfriends, pop music...*

"I was fourteen when my mother died. She died because... what do you call it when a group of young men rob people?"

There was a quiet exchange with the translator: *banda; pandilla callejera.*

"A gang, yes. My brothers were grown and gone. I lived with my mother and her husband, but he was nothing to me. He had just finished building a house, and they paid him in cash. This gang, they knew we had cash in the house. They only wanted to rob us. They even knocked first.

"My mother opened the door.

"I don't think they had thought to kill her, but when she saw the guns, she tried to push the door closed, and they pushed back. I guess they realized my mother had seen their faces and they couldn't just leave."

Luisa looked to the door again, and shifted in her seat. Her face became agitated.

"I was in the back room when I heard the shot. I ran out, and there was my mother on the floor." Luisa cried out as if her mother's body lay before her all over again. "My mother! All of her blood. What's happening? What's happening??" Her breathing was quick and labored.

"The guy is standing over my mother with his gun, and the other guys are around him. He looks up. He sees I see him! He sees I know what he did. I wait for him to shoot me, too."

Instead, the ragtag group ran away. They left unfinished business.

"My brothers came and stayed the Nine Days. We prayed. We prayed for my mother's soul."

Luisa is referring to *novena*, a Catholic tradition in which family members stay together and pray together for nine days after a relative's funeral.

"A few days later, I was with my brothers in my mother's house when I heard someone outside calling my name. I went out to see. It was one of the older ones from the gang. As soon as he saw me, he said, 'You saw. You *saw.*'" Her lip curled, imitating his growling threat. "He says, 'If you tell anyone who you saw, we will kill you, *and* we will kill your brothers.'

"I turned and ran into the house. I found my oldest brother, and I told him everything. My brother said, 'Sister, who was it said that? Where is he?' I pointed to the window, but he went and looked and said, 'He's gone!' We were all very afraid.

"The next day, I left with my older brother to live with him and his wife far away in another city."

"What city?" I said, but Luisa shook her head, afraid to name it.

"Three months later, I was outside on the street, and that same guy showed up. He had others with him. They got out of the car and surrounded me. I shook so hard. That first guy, he got up close to my face, and he said, 'We think you'll talk.'

"I said, 'No, no, señor! I won't say anything!'
He said, 'Yes, you will.' I said, 'I won't!'

"I turned and ran into the house. I don't know
why they let me go. I don't know why they just
stood there and watched.

"When my brother came home, he looked at
me and said, 'Sister, what is the matter with you?'
I said, 'Nothing.' He said, 'Sister, look at you!
What is it?' but I wouldn't tell. If I did, maybe he
would say I couldn't stay with him anymore.

"I stayed inside the house for months. I didn't
go out anywhere, and all the time I kept the curtains
closed. Then I turned fifteen. I got brave. I decided
I could go do errands, so I did, just like that... and
they got me. They drove up and jumped out and
dragged me into their car.

"They are the ones — the fathers of my son."

The impossible plural in Luisa's words seared
the air between us.

"A letter came to my brother's house. They wrote,
'She's going to talk, and when she does, we will
kill you.' Then another one came that said the same
thing, and another.

"After maybe a year and a half of the letters, I
took my son with me and went to live in Santa Rosa
de Lima. I wanted us to start over in a new place. I
was seventeen."

Luisa had moved closer to the area where she grew up. Santa Rosa de Lima is a short bus ride from San Miguel.

"There I met the man who became my husband. He built us a *campecita* — a little camping house — behind his mother's house so that we could be alone, but it had a real roof, good and strong. We cooked in his mother's house, but we lived and slept out in the *campecita*."

Thus, Luisa, who grew up in a city apartment complex with two parents and a regular income, public schools, running water, electricity, and a lock on the door, became a *campesina*.

"I was happy. Then my mother-in-law started to treat me badly. It got so I was afraid to be around her. My son was growing, and she said she resented him eating her food like he was her family.

"Where else could I go? I couldn't go back to my brother; the gang was sending him letters every week.

"You know, my husband, he was kind. He kept himself all the time between my mother-in-law and me. I decided we were all right. I had another baby, a boy, when I was eighteen.

"When the little one was a year old, my husband's mother said we couldn't keep living off her. There was no work. My husband left to

Estados Unidos to find work there. He promised to send money.

"Two years passed. All that time he sent only a little. I stayed with the boys in our *campecita*, but his mother kept saying she didn't want us on her property, and she only gave us food when my husband sent money. I washed clothes for people. I did any work I could find. Sometimes I begged. Still, there were days when we didn't eat.

My husband stopped sending any money, and he didn't call any more. His mother wouldn't give us food or even look at the boy she said wasn't her family; she only talked to the little one. Finally, I said, 'No more.'

"I called my husband's brother in Houston. He's a Christian, and I felt he would help. I told him, 'I know my husband has an Americana now. I will come to *Estados Unidos* and work for my boys myself.'

"He said, 'Sister, do you have the courage?'

"And I said, 'Yes.'

"I knew my mother-in-law would take care of the younger one. Next day, I took my older boy and our few things, and I left for my brother's house.

"When I got there, my brother told me, 'They know you're here. I got another letter.'

"I asked what they said. He told me, 'They say you'll talk.'

"I told him I had to leave. I told him I was going to *Estados Unidos*, and I asked him to take care of my son.

"Next day, I told my friend who lived next door to my brother that I was leaving. She was also a long-suffering person, also waiting too long for her husband to send for her. She said, 'Are you really going?' I said, 'Yes,' and she said, 'I'll go with you.' She had tried to go to *Estados Unidos* three times before, but the *migras* [immigration patrol] always caught her.

"I was so happy. I'd been afraid to go by myself. I thought, *God is helping me.*

"I sold my things. I took the money I got, and we left."

For a single illogical moment in our very different lives, in my eyes Luisa and I became just two mothers who had both once turned, chin down, face belying nothing, and walked away from our children carrying that terrible phantom-limb feeling, even though when I left, I could tell myself that my two boys still at home were safe and I would see them soon and often.

I looked at Luisa and knew that she knew what she broke in her boys by leaving. I knew at least in some small part what it must have taken for her to keep walking away.

"We crossed El Salvador by bus. We were going first to Guatemala.

"At a stop near the border, we saw someone who looked like a gentleman, but he came up too close and said in a low voice, 'You are not from here.' He said, 'Are you going to *el otro lado?*' [the other side, that is, the United States.]

"I didn't like his manner. We knew what happened too often to women like us. We said, 'No!' and quickly walked away. After that, we decided, if we had to ask anyone anything, we would only ask a woman.

"At our first stop in Guatemala, we asked someone if that bus was going to Mexico, and she said, 'Take that one there.' We continued across Guatemala like that; always, we only asked women.

At a bus terminal when we were about to cross over into Mexico, my friend got very scared and said, 'We're running out of money!' I said, 'Come on. We'll go into town. We'll wash clothes or beg. Something.' I told her, 'I'll go ask that man where the next bus goes,' and I did — I asked him."

She chose to ask a man. It was as if Luisa was telling her friend, *Trust me — I can get us all the help we need, and I can tell who is safe to ask!*

"The man said, 'Are you by yourselves? Aren't you afraid?' I told him, 'No, I'm not afraid,' and he said, 'Come to my house and work for my wife for a couple of days. You can help her make cheese, make a little money, and then continue on.'

"I don't know why I knew to trust him. I just knew, and it worked! The man and his wife gave us work and food and a place to sleep. It turned out they had done this for many people.

"Then my friend started to feel sick. She got in the bed the woman made up for us, and soon she had fever, and it began to rain very hard. I looked at my friend and then outside at the rain and I thought, *My God. What if she can't go on? I can't do this by myself.*"

However determined she was, and continued to be, the only time in Luisa's story before this that she had gone out alone, she was attacked. The trembling in her voice returned.

"My friend started talking through the fever, saying stuff about her kids. She had a two-year-old boy, a nine-year-old girl, and another girl fourteen, and another one eighteen and married.

Luisa was trying to talk through tears.

"I told her not to cry. I told her not to get that way because I didn't want to cry for my kids. Then we both started. I told her, 'We will get to *el otro lado*,' but she said, 'I can't.' I heard myself say, 'If you won't, I will do it without you. If they catch me, I'll turn around and go again no matter how many times I have to try. I will make it into *Estados Unidos* where I can bring my children and keep them safe.'

"Later, I asked the woman who took us in if she thought I could make it by myself. She told me, 'I can see that you're strong enough.'

"I asked her husband to show me where to get the next bus and where each bus went after that, and if he would draw a map and mark everything, which he did. He gave me fifty pesos for my work [about two and a half US dollars]. I said, 'I can make it with this,' and I left.

"All this happened in southern Mexico. At the bus stop near the house where I left my friend, I moved close to a group of women and I said, very quietly, 'Do you know which bus that one is?'

"They heard my accent. One of them said, 'You are not from here.'

Luisa squared her shoulders and narrowed her eyes. Her tone became defiant. "I said, 'No, I'm not from here.'"

The woman softened, as did Luisa's voice. "She whispered, 'Get this next bus.'

"She wrote down the names of all the checkpoints for me. Mexico had checkpoints all over the country to catch people like me. She said the next bus was going to Oaxaca, the next state, and she said, 'Be careful not to look nervous.'

"I thanked her, and I got on.

"After that, whenever the bus stopped at a checkpoint, I took out a magazine and pretended to fix my hair and put on makeup, and the whole time I told myself, don't get nervous. It worked. Whenever guards got on, they passed right by me, and they didn't even look. I was wearing a long skirt, not pants or tennis shoes that might look like I was ready to do a lot of walking, and I didn't carry a suitcase — just a bag with underwear in it. Every time an officer passed me by and got back off the bus, I said, 'Oh, thank you, God.' In this way, I arrived in Arriaga in Chiapas State, in south Mexico. I hadn't gotten to Oaxaca yet, but I had to change buses. I got off."

Border towns like Arriaga are notorious for brothels that are staffed by migrant women and appear to be restaurants. Women traveling through the area are often kidnapped and forced into this work, especially if they're traveling alone.

"I got on the next bus and took a seat, but the lady next to me kept staring at me. We came to a federal checkpoint, not just a local one, and this time, federal officers came down the aisle saying, 'Papers, papers.'

"I started shaking so hard that the officer stopped and looked at me. He said, 'Are you from here?'

"I couldn't help it. I knew he could tell. I said, 'No, señor.' He told me to get off right now."

Luisa was shaking again. It seemed she looked at me but didn't see me.

"He walked me a little way from the bus before he said, 'Why are you crying?'

"I said, 'I have nothing. They killed my mother. I left my babies.'

"He looked serious. He said, 'That's why you're crying?'

"I said, 'Yes. Now you will send me back after everything I went through, and I'll have to start over.' I knew I would start over. I knew I wouldn't stop trying.

He said, 'Don't cry. Who said that I'll arrest you?' He put his hand in his pocket and pulled out one hundred Mexican pesos.

"I said, 'Oh, thank you, señor!' I wiped at the tears. He told me to get back on the bus."

"The same lady sat next to me. After we had traveled a while, she said quietly, 'Do you plan to cross over?' I nodded 'yes.' We rode a long time. Then she stood to leave, and I asked if she knew where there was a hotel. She said, 'Is anyone expecting you?' "I shook my head 'no.' She leaned closer and said, 'Come to my house.'"

Certainly, that woman knew about the terrible coyote guides that dominated the area, and their pre-paid 'arrangements.' She knew she could put herself in mortal danger by interfering in their business.

"I said to myself, *Lord, you put this woman here for me.*"

"They lived in a fishing village by the sea. She had a little house with her husband and two daughters. He fished shrimp. She cleaned them and sold them. She asked if I had eaten; then she told her husband she'd found someone to take care of the girls for a couple of days while she worked. He welcomed me and said his wife would help me to cross over.

"I liked him. I asked him, 'Do you really think I can make it?' I needed him to say yes. Whenever I'd asked someone before this how to get to Matamoros [a border town where many go to cross over] they shook their heads and say, 'They'll rape you there. They'll kill you.'

"The woman answered before her husband. She said, 'You'll make it; I can see it in your face.' I told her my husband had gone to *los Estados Unidos*, but then he got with an *Americana*. She said, never mind, that she was certain I would make it on my own.

"I spent three days in that house. In the last hour, the woman took my picture, then she took me to the mayor's office and paid for a fake birth certificate so I could get through the rest of the checkpoints. When she gave me the certificate, she said, 'I'll go with you through the first checkpoint. At that one, they're very strict because it's near Mexico City. You'll have to ask God to help us get through.'

"Next day, we got up very early. She gave me money, and what I'd like to tell you is, on the bus, she put her hand on my arm and said, 'We're coming to a checkpoint. Stay calm. I'll ask you questions, and you answer and laugh.'

"Two officers got on the bus, and right away she started chatting and sounding happy, saying, 'Are you excited? Did you remember to pack a toothbrush? What are you going to do first when you get there?' and the officers passed us right by! They asked everyone on the bus but me for papers.

"Then we got to the next stop, where you get a bus to Mexico City, and we both got off. She said, 'God's going to bless you from here.'

"Before she left, she said, 'Be sure to show the birth certificate when you buy your ticket, and you need more money.' She started to walk away, then she turned and waved, and she mouthed, *God bless..*

"I called my friend in Houston and told her that when I got to Mexico City, I was going to need one hundred dollars for another ticket. I told her that only a Mexican resident was allowed to receive money by wire, and I was afraid to claim the money myself because I would have to show the fake birth certificate. She said, 'I'll send the money. Ask one of the agents at the ticket window to accept it for you.'"

In Mexico City, I looked for a few minutes before I picked out a woman in one of the ticket booths. I went up to her and said, 'Could you do me a favor?'

"She said, 'What do you want?'

"I said, 'I was sent a Western Union wire for a hundred dollars, but I need someone who can claim it.'

"She asked where I was going. I said, 'Matamoros,' and she said, 'You are not from here.'"

Luisa would not accept that epithet any more.

"I said, 'Señora, please do me this favor!'

"She sighed and said, 'Wait for lunchtime when I can go out.'

"I sat and waited on a bench for almost an hour. I knew she could just claim the money and keep it, but finally she showed up, and she said, 'Here's your hundred dollars.' I was smiling! Then I took a deep breath and told her that I also needed to buy a ticket.

"The woman raised her eyebrows, but I just handed her the fake birth certificate, and she didn't question it! She went into the booth and made me a ticket to Matamoros. She handed it to me and said, 'You depart at three o'clock.'"

"While I was waiting for the bus, a man came over and asked me where I was going. I didn't like him. I said, 'Nowhere,' and then, 'I'm waiting for a friend,' and I turned away.

"He said, 'You're a wetback.'"

That's a common pejorative. Inside the States, the term implied Luisa was still wet from swimming the Rio Grande that defines the Texas/Mexico border. The term also implied she was unwanted, not from here.

Luisa took that as a threat. She said, with a sneer, "No, I'm not! Don't you see that I'm dry?"

"Then the man moved too close. He said he could get me to the other side. He said, 'You won't pay a lot.'

"They announced the bus to Matamoros. I walked away fast and got on the bus. I was glad that where I sat down, the seat next to me was taken, but he followed me onto the bus, and then he came down the aisle. When he got to me, he said, 'Oh, you were waiting for a friend, were you? You just didn't want to come with me.'

Luisa imitated his taunting manner.

"I turned and stared out the window until he went away."

"When the bus stopped, I had fallen asleep. I didn't hear the driver call out the name on my fake birth certificate. 'Jovita Perez, we are at the bathrooms!' I opened my eyes, and the driver was standing over me. He said, 'You are not Jovita Perez, are you?'

"I had to think; I had to wake up. I said, 'I am!' but I could see he didn't believe me.

"He said, 'Show me your birth certificate.'

"I did. He read it and said, 'Wellll, you *are* Jovita Perez. So... how old are you?'

"I said, 'Thirty-two.'

"He said, 'You don't look thirty-two.' Then, he just let it go!

"At another checkpoint, I showed the officer my ID, and he said, 'Are you from here?' I looked at him and said my name and age exactly as it was on the paper."

Coyote: a sly, fast, vicious creature adept at moving in on its kill in moonlight. Also, a smuggler of human beings.

"In Matamoros, a woman came up to me and said, 'You are not from here.' I didn't answer her. She whispered, 'I'm a Christian. Do you need help?'

"I decided to trust her.

"We walked half an hour from the terminal, and she brought me to a house where I stayed two days. Then a man came who said he would bring me over the border. He called my brother-in-law and told him, 'If you want her to walk, you pay fifteen hundred dollars to get her over the line.' *Over the line* meant you already had papers so you could go over the border like you were just going to see a friend. It meant you didn't have to cross the river.

"I didn't have papers, but my brother-in-law said, 'Take her over the line. Do it. I'll send the money,' and right away, my brother-in-law sent half. The other half he said he'd give them when I got there."

Then Luisa was getting ready for the march, wondering where all the food was for the journey and who was going to carry it, and eyeing the men who were to be her companions.

"I asked how long we were going to walk, and the man said, 'About six hours.' Then he said my shoes would never hold up. He took them away and gave me used tennis shoes that were too small with no laces in them, and we set out. There were six men and me."

This is how invested Luisa was in believing the coyote's promises: she ignored her instincts, now so well-honed, and gave up her good shoes, then this woman who had been gangraped set out alone with six men she did not know into an uninhabited area. There could not have been a clearer illustration of Luisa's desperation to get to work, shelter, and safety — her definition of American freedom.

Late that night, the group stepped into the Rio Grande at the southern tip of Texas. The water where they crossed was relatively shallow, their actual crossing strangely silent beneath a universe of stars in a black sky. This was before a steel-girded wall slashed the area, and before tent cities formed on the Mexican side of the border filled with thousands of people hoping and waiting. Border security was sparse in those days. There were no witnesses to their crossing, save one another, and there was no time or means to mark this transition other than in memory. Very soon, eight people stepped out of the water on the Other Side into a future that would be forever divided for them between *before* and *after*, between home and *el Otro Lado*. Among them, one woman. The group looked at one another without comment and set out to walk the valley formed by the great river. For a short time, they left a wet, fading trail behind them.

"We walked all that night and then three long days, always going the wrong way along the road, with the traffic instead of against it. That way, if someone passed, they couldn't see our faces. Whenever we heard a car coming, we ran and jumped over a fence. We slept on the ground near whatever little shelter we could find — a fence or a tree. We had paid fifteen hundred dollars for bad shoes, and water and crackers for food.

"By the third day, my legs were scratched from the cacti near the highway. My feet had bleeding sores from the shoes, and my ankles were so swollen that if I did have laces I would not have been able to close the shoes."

A large number of North America's migrating birds pass over this fertile area between the southwest desert and the Gulf of Mexico. Some of the birds settle for the winter in sanctuaries on the Texas coast. Others continue into Central and South America, using the shore as a sightline. The birds will return on the same route, drawn by the hope of spring.

Here is Luisa in a long skirt and open sneakers amid six men as dirty as she. Her skin is sunburned, her eyes red, something raw and fierce in her face. She puts one foot in front of the other again and again in a numbed relentless march. Seen from above, the group melts into a river of movement, every living thing above and below headed north.

They begin to run, until they come to a barbed wire fence. Luisa looks at the men wild-eyed. The men surround her and lift her over. They follow, to crouch together invisible in the overgrowth. Around Luisa, labored breathing, the smells of fresh dirt and unwashed bodies, rustle of dry grass in the wind. Somewhere a crow caws. A police car whizzes by. It shrinks down the gray ribbon of road that runs through a hundred miles of farmland and disappears.

They wait. A flock of geese passes overhead in a shifting V. Then the group climbs back over and resumes their trek. They wish for wings.

"It was just me and the men. I kept myself apart and asked God all day to protect me and help me.

"After we walked most of a day, we came to a wall, and the guide said we had to wait there. We waited there for three days. We had crackers and water and no shade. It was very hot.

The next day, one of the men threw up, and after that he could only lie down. My stomach started to feel hard. My mouth was dry. I just wanted to sleep. You know you can die; you stop caring about what will happen. I started to believe no one was going to come for us."

"I woke in the middle of the night and found snakes crawling over my legs. They were all over all of us. I screamed and screamed. The guide pulled out garlic and yelled at us to crush the cloves fast and rub them on our shoes and skin."

Deadly cottonmouth and rattlers are the most common snakes in that area.

"It worked; the snakes went away and they stayed away."

"The third night, the guide woke us up and said we had to get up and start walking. It felt like a dream. It was so dark out we couldn't see. I don't know how we kept moving or how we stayed together. We knew the area was patrolled by immigration. We could see the shape of a wall in the distance along a highway because of the lights.

"We came to a big tree and stopped there for eight hours. By now we were all sick.

"None of us could sleep. Sitting there in the dark, the guide said he was worried about me. He said, 'Listen. In the morning, you're going to see a truck, and you're going to have to run very fast and jump over the wall to get in. I don't see how you can do it.'

"*Oh*, I thought, *he's right*. I was weak, and my ankles were so swollen.

He told everyone, 'Listen up! The truck will honk twice. By the third honk, you better be in it.'

"I looked around at the men. All that way, I had kept myself apart. I hadn't spoken a word to any of them. I picked one, and I said, 'Señor, will you help me?' and he said, 'Don't you worry.'

"That's how it was: a truck came, and when it honked the second time, a few of the men grabbed me and lifted me over the wall, and the whole time they were saying, 'It's coming, it's coming!' They rushed so much to get us all over that wall that some of them tore their shirts and their arms got scratched and bleeding, and I fell over the top, but some of the others were on the other side and they caught me. They caught me! They pulled me fast into the truck.

"That truck, it was like a farm truck to carry produce to market, with high wooden sides. The cab had a back seat, but we were eight people. The men lay on top of each other on the floor in the back and on the floor in front, but there still wasn't enough room. The driver told me and one of the men to get under his knees near the pedals and not to move.

"I got right down near the floor in front of him and the guy lay on top of me — at least he was small and didn't crush me — but I said, 'Please, would you please let me go on top?' He said, 'Okay, señora. Main thing is we get there.'

"No one moved. No one spoke. We rode like that for hours. Finally, we came to Victoria, Texas, and the driver yelled, 'Here's a store. There's food!'

I had been traveling twenty-eight days, in the same clothes.

"They called my brother-in-law. He came right away from Houston in his car; it took about an hour for him to get there. When he saw me alive, he gave the coyote the rest of the money."

Generations of migrants were churning in me, our great need for refuge. I wanted to hold up my hand and tell Luisa, *You can stop now*. I wanted this to be the end of her journey and for it to be a good ending. I wanted to be able to say, *What you've been through is enough. You've come home.*

We're home.

"In my brother-in-law's house, I took a shower and washed my clothes, and I tried to eat. Then, I slept. I slept a very long time.

"When I woke up, I called my husband. I didn't tell him where I was. I just said, 'Hi. How are you?'

"He was surprised to hear my voice. He said, 'Uh... and... you?' Then, he got angry. He really started yelling. He said, 'My mother said you left our son. No one knew where you were!'

"His mother had told him that I had run off with another man and abandoned my children.

"I just listened, and he calmed down. I said I needed money, and he said he would send it. Then, I don't know what he was telling his lover in English, but I said, 'Do you have the courage to tell that Americana it's your *wife* on the phone?'

"He got very quiet. I said, 'I need the money now.'

"He said, 'Okay. Where do I send it?'

"I said, 'I'm in Houston.'"

"For three months, he kept asking me to forgive him. He called, he came over, he bought me gifts, and finally, I did. I don't know why I forgave him. I didn't have anybody else, just him.

"We thought we could bring our boys and make a life here. I wanted it to be like when we were in our little *campecita* in Salvador, but without his mother. I thought it could be like that."

"Every month, we sent money to my mother-in-law and to my brother to take care of our boys, but when I called to talk to my son who was with my brother, my brother said he wasn't there. It started to worry me.

"My husband's brother who lives in Houston has papers; he is allowed to travel. He went to El Salvador, and he called me from there. He said, 'You have to get your son out of here.' He said my brother wasn't giving the boy food if we didn't send money. He said, when I called, my brother made my son hang up.

"We had to bring the boys right away, but we already had used every penny we could to send money to support them. We'd even borrowed.

"What could we do? We just kept working until we had saved enough to bring them.

"When we finally had the money, we called my brother. He said he knew a woman who would do it. He said they'd only put my son in a trailer for four hours at the end of the trip and he wouldn't have to walk, and that the boy would never go without food. It all went fine. He's fine. It cost us six thousand five hundred dollars. We brought him here in October."

It was a staggering amount. Then I thought, *Fine? Could he really be fine?*

"We worked hard, and we were able to bring the younger boy the following April. They brought him in a trailer too, and then on a bus, but he was only eight, and they made him walk many hours.

For twelve days, they kept handing him over to different guides. Every time the guide changed, the new one called and demanded more money. I worried so much. One of them took our son with him in the box under an eighteen-wheel truck — there's a shelf underneath near the engine for spare tires. They got in between the tires. When the truck gets moving, the noise and vibration are terrible. A grown man can get shaken off. We've known so many who died on this road — raped and their throats cut, or robbed then shot, or they died when they fell off the trains or trucks.

"The man and my son made it over the border. Then, he handed my son off to someone else. The last guide was supposed to bring him to Houston. We were supposed to pay after we got him, but he called and said my son was too smart, and he talked too much. He said, 'Send me another five thousand dollars.'

"I panicked. I said, 'You're supposed to bring him here to me first!'

"He said, 'If you want to see your son alive again, you will send the money now.'

"It was Thursday. I paid rent and sent him half of what he wanted. That's all I had. Then, nothing.

"Friday, April 29, I got a call from Border Patrol saying they had my son. The coyote left him there, then he gave them my name and telephone number and disappeared. Immigration would only give him up to a relative with the same last name.

My son — we're lucky the coyote didn't kill him.

"Many of my husband's relatives are here in Houston, and they all have papers. We tried to get one of them to go for my son because they have the same last name. We also asked friends who have papers; they're legal, they should be able to go to Border Patrol, and no one should make trouble for them, but everyone was afraid of the *migras*. Not one friend or relative would go for my son. I gave myself up to claim him."

Luisa's husband was bitter that his family would not help them claim their son. He felt that, on principal, family had to help family.

I couldn't breathe when Luisa told me this, couldn't speak. I marveled that it was she who went to claim the boy, the only one of the two of them who faced a murder threat if she were to be sent back to El Salvador. Her husband stayed behind and let her go. This is how naïve I was: I had thought that by leaving the Hasidim I had left behind men who posture dominance and offer women no protection, and men who thought a child solely a woman's responsibility regardless of the risk. Another little piece of my naivety fell away.

It was 2005. When Luisa got to the border and made her petition, they released her son to her.

Relieved, she returned to Houston with him, papers in hand.

"Now most nights my youngest dreams he is under the truck, and he wakes up screaming. This story he will live every day of his life. I must remember that we're lucky both our boys are alive. We thank God every day. As for me, all I have now is this order for deportation."

They went to YMCA International, which sponsors refugees, for help. They went to CARECEN — the Central American Resource Center, which offers legal support. Lawyer friends of the opera company got involved, but everyone said the same thing: Luisa had crossed the border without a permit. They said, if she had a work permit before entering, she could remain here and keep the boy with her since he was a minor and her dependent. But she didn't. They said a judge would consider the gang's threat of murder to be El Salvador's 'internal problem' and deny her asylum. Besides, they said, the US was no longer granting asylum to Salvadorans.

"If they send me back, where will I go? My mother-in-law sold our *campecita*. After what my brother did to my son, I can't go back to him, either."

Then, she brightened. It seemed Luisa trusted that American judges would bend the law to keep it human. This was her home now; she clung to her dream of America, land of justice. Land of refuge.

"I know what I'll do! I have the newspaper clipping about the gang that murdered my mother. I brought it with me in my bag. I'll show that to the judge and tell him he *has* to give me protection!"

The space between us felt weighted. Then, Luisa's eyes narrowed with a hint of anger.

"If they send me back, I will start over. I can do it. I know I can do it, because now I know how."

In the end, it seemed a shade went down over Luisa's face. I thanked her and the translator, snapped the case shut on my equipment, and made my way out to the car.

Outside on the curved drive of that house on a hill, I fastened my seatbelt and lowered the window to the scent of roses when suddenly, Luisa's shaking voice was there in my mind saying she had always been afraid before that day to tell anyone her story. I thought, *Then she signed an agreement to tell the world by telling me.*

What had changed? Why was she willing to talk when she never dared before? Then, a surge of sad surprise, and I realized how desperate Luisa's hope was that we could help her.

This was my first real confrontation with the moral ambiguities embedded in this work. I had just taken Luisa's story for my own use without noting how little she would gain by giving it, or the pain the telling might cause her, or that it was possible that some great need drove her to tell me. I had failed to note that working with the opera company might imply that I had power I didn't have and had ignored the imbalance of power between us. I had seen Luisa's fear during the interview as something I needed to gently overcome, then I simply thanked her and left.

Until that moment on a hill in a Houston spring breeze, I had thought of my writing as a statement of my glorious new freedom, had felt my fabled American freedom of speech as an exultation after years in a censored world. I thought then, *No one can ever again tell me what to write or what not to write.* Now I realized how this naïve, unbridled exuberance, this lack of self-monitoring, could become predatory. Luisa had just re-experienced her mother's murder and her own rape because of this work. Because I urged her to break her silence, the death threats she fled will now echo even more. Just by listening, I had fed her impossible hope.

The wall between me and my subjects, a wall of cool professionality, of craft, came tumbling down. I resolved to check my motives repeatedly and never push anyone to talk again. Before anyone began to speak, I would explain exactly what they would and would not gain, and then pay close attention to how the speaker was handling the telling. I would be ready and willing to stop at any time if it seemed they needed to do so. My hand shook as I turned the key in the ignition, as I pulled out of the driveway and headed to my apartment.

As I drove, a litany of loss filled my mind like a singsong.

Luisa left her boys. She left her family, her friends, her society, her web of support. She left her only language, and the people she loved who expressed themselves as she did. She left all the ways in which she communicated without words, and the people who understood her. She left her home to be exiled in language, crippled in it.

Luisa left the music of home that soothed her with memories of childhood. She left work -- income. She left *food*. She left electricity, running water, and shelter; she set out to manage without these things for as long as it would take to get to safety.

She left citizenship in the country of her birth — the right to eat and sleep and live in a place without challenge. She left any protection of law, such that it was. She left her home knowing that there were sexual predators on her route. She set out penniless and exposed.

It was as if the civil war had never stopped, as if it continued to spin through her country, flinging its people away. I saw Luisa as a war survivor, and rape as the classic war crime, the ultimate statement of victory. The women raped on that route were fallen soldiers no one honored.

In time, another interview subject would tell me of a wry, all-too-common slang term used by migrants like Luisa: *cuerpomatica*, or "body machine." Stated in the feminine form, the word evoked a picture of a woman's body as an ATM, a machine with no feeling used as a tool to pay. Women used the term casually, as if rape was the inevitable cost of the journey.

Driving home that day in the late slant of sunlight, Luisa's 'I know how' grew into a huge wave of men and women in a march across the landscape, an inexorable drive toward life and away from death that no government could stop. Again, she was saying, 'If they send me back, I'll just come again.'

I wanted to remember each of the people who helped Luisa along her way. I imagined each as part of an underground railroad formed for all of the Luisas. There were the women at a bus stop who gave her directions, and the policeman who reached into his own pocket to help, the man who brought her to his home, and his wife who gave Luisa work and welcome and care, and the woman who risked her own safety to accompany Luisa through a dangerous checkpoint and then showered her with blessings. There was the woman at the ticket booth in Mexico City, and the six men who lifted her over a wall and into the truck that brought them to safety.

Here was Luisa that day early in the journey when she looked outside at a downpour and realized that her friend could not continue and that she would have to go on alone. Luisa turned to her benefactor then, and only with that woman's reassurance was she able to set out again. Those who helped along the way were her scaffold. Ahead, the United States beckoned, promising to be the ultimate helping hand.

Across nineteen hundred miles to Houston, Luisa held onto her bag, inside it, a change of underwear, a coin purse, and a newspaper clipping reporting her mother's murder. Luisa believed throughout her trek that the news article would constitute proof to any official with a heart that she had to be granted asylum. She clung to this proof. She believed my country had that heart, and its officials would listen.

In the weeks leading up to her court date, I often pictured Luisa handing the judge that ragged clipping. I imagined the look on her face, her loss of faith, her sudden aging, when the judge waved it away and she was forced to confront her own naivety.

Five years before Luisa went to the border to claim her son, George W. Bush had replaced the

US Immigration and Naturalization Service with ICE — Immigration and Customs Enforcement. That shift, from using the terms 'naturalization' and 'service' to 'enforcement,' signaled a sea change in the United States, from processing paperwork for immigrants to criminalizing them. By the time I met Luisa, anyone who crossed the border without papers was no longer someone who needed to get their documents in order, no longer a needy human in search of work, food, and safety who was welcome to wait in line and jump through the proper hoops. Now they were criminals.

If all of this were to happen just a few years later than it did, there would be no impending court date. Neither would Luisa have a deportation order, or even imagine that telling me her story might be of help. Instead, Luisa's son would be in caged detention. If she foolishly showed her face to Immigration and Customs Enforcement, they would send her back to El Salvador almost immediately, without the boy and with little chance of seeing him again.

The opera company consulted various immigration lawyers on Luisa's behalf, but they all said there was nothing they could do. They advised her that when the day came, the judge would uphold the deportation order.

I never did find out what happened to Luisa and her little family after that, flung as they were from a country broken by war. I felt that the impact of that journey would continue through generations of her family. I imagined Luisa left marked with ghostly outlines of her mother, brothers, aunts, uncles, cousins, and neighbors left behind, overlain with heavier outlines of the unnamed men who had assaulted her — all faces that would ping through her body and appear in dreams. I imagined she would left with aversions, odd habits, perhaps a tendency to long silences that would impact in a thousand unexplained ways the lives of those who needed her.

After telling me her story, would she resume refusing to talk about *before* to anyone?

All Luisa wanted — and all my family once wanted — was safety; shelter; a place where she wouldn't be alone before the onslaught of the world.

It is said that beneath the forest floor, tree roots reach out and merge with underground roots of other trees despite type, creating miles and miles of buried filaments that function as an underground communication network that stretches throughout the forest. Through these filaments, trees share warnings and protection and food, and feed the sick and dying. Which is why, in an old forest, trees live hundreds and even thousands of years longer than when they're isolated and alone.

Luisa had wanted a place in the forest.

A great pool of people rocketed from their countries swirled around me while I wrote the opera. I worked in that vortex, to the drumbeat of Luisa's steady walking and the approach and retreat of great crashing waves. As I worked, a voice from my family sang in me, saying, *Of course these people came here. The United States has always been a place where a newcomer can be just one more remnant of a family from somewhere else.* I thought, *But that isn't true.*

What does it mean to be of a place? To become of a place? There was a time when I would have shrugged off the question as irrelevant, when I took for granted the notion of the United States as my home, as if my family had always been a part of this country. Now the question vibrated in me. I argued with it, countered with *But I'm from here.* I was born in the United States, I was raised here, as were my parents. I dream and feel in American English. My gestures and tastes and appearance are reflected in those around me. I don't need to understand what it means to become an American — I am of this place. And yet, some knowledge in my cells kept me scanning the horizon for refuge, ready to fly, as if I had never been truly rooted.

In this way, I teetered between past and present, 'from here' and 'not from here,' all the while holding these stories to my chest as I danced with poor balance on the tiny hyphen that held together my hyphenated identity, stuck in a contradictory impossible self-portrait so common I thought it just might be quintessentially American. This was the beginning of my belonging.

In the end, the 'you are not from here' that Luisa encountered so many times on her journey recurred in the opera like a drumbeat. I ended her movement on the great rising assertion of her words: 'If they send me back, I will start again, because now I know how.'

The Refuge was set to debut a short time before the date that Luisa was supposed to surrender to Immigration. I had nothing to offer her of what she needed. I could only hope that maybe, if she sat in the dark hall one night, she might catch the moment when she was surrounded by thousands listening to her story as one heart, joined with her song. Maybe for that one evening she could feel of a place that at least for the moment embraced her. *The Refuge* would be one more hand proffered on her journey, a few words of encouragement, and I would be just another on her route offering some small kindness before she continued on.

Each of my subjects was to be met before the performance and escorted to their seats. Sue Elliott of the opera company, who had shepherded me through so much of this project, arranged for a translation of the libretto into Spanish and promised to have a copy ready. She assured me that she would meet Luisa herself and personally escort her to her seat.

Two days before the opening, I remembered the dots on the dress Luisa wore the day we met and mentioned to my wife that those photographs had gone to costuming. We looked at one another in horror. I ran to the phone and called Sue in a panic. "Tell Luisa not to wear the polka-dotted dress!"

That night as the curtain rose, my mind was on one small-boned woman in the sea of an audience I had dubbed 'Luisa' who could hear the production as a mirror of song held up before her, exactly as Freud had imagined and yet like nothing either of us could have imagined, before she slipped out into the streets for home.

I often thought of Luisa's boys after that, the younger one with his nightmares and the older one who Luisa had said was fine. Whenever I passed an eighteen-wheeler on a freeway, I noted the cage of enormous tires beneath like the one in which her son had come, and that took me to my refugee grandparents as children, starved and vomiting in steerage of a cargo ship; the rocking and long fearful days. I wanted to hear that Luisa's son didn't suffer nightmares like his brother, and no white-hot flashes of fear or anger that tore at people he loved as he grew, like my grandfather. I wanted to believe Luisa when she said that at least one of her boys was fine. With the terror bound up with her secret, would she, *could* she, help them? Did she show up on the appointed date, or did she disappear back into life *sin papeles?* I never found out. The soprano song that was Luisa remained in me, Luisa herself an ever-receding figure, her two boys at either side.

Every year, over a million people are apprehended trying to cross our southern border. More than a million others get through.

El Salvador remains haunted with ghosts of *campesino* rebels, of roving death squads, and of the thousands of the disappeared, the beloved landscape dotted with mass graves. Gangs still mirror the tactics of those death squads of old —

the next generation of war-wounded exacting their revenge on anyone with money. The women are their pawns.

Intermezzo

Voices

Woman from El Salvador:
"I was the oldest of eight kids, and there was always too much work. I had to stop school after fifth grade to help my mother at home and my father in the cornfield, but maybe I didn't do enough because when I was thirteen, my mother sent me away to clean house for a rich family in San Salvador. I lived with them three years, slept in the kitchen, only worked — nothing more. I had no time for friends. Every month, they paid me fifty *colones* [about twelve dollars]. I sent it all home."

Man from El Salvador:
"They put fifty of us in a trailer. It was so hot inside that we all passed out from the heat. There was no air, but they stopped and opened the door and found us. They slapped our faces, brought us back. Then, they changed us to another van."

From El Salvador:
"My husband had permanent status here, but he wasn't allowed to bring his wife."

From Mexico:
"I got married to someone who was born here. He gave me the first black eye three months later. I'd seen a lot of husbands beating up their wives back home, but stupid me, I had thought, he's Anglo, he calls himself a Christian. He'll be different.

"He used to tell me, 'You're Mexican — you're worthless. No one will help you here.'"

Woman from Pakistan:
"I'm a physician. I came here, and I went to work in an emergency room. Many times, I treated women who had been beaten by their husbands. Oh yes, Pakistan is full of that, but innocent me, I didn't expect to find it here."

From El Salvador:
"My husband was a very angry man. When I left him, he threw my immigration papers in the trash. Anyway, only he could sign them. I had filed my application, but everything came to his house. Me and my daughter... suddenly I had no work, no papers, no car, and no house. I found us a place, and I found work cleaning houses. Fifteen years later, I

got a work permit, and after twenty, I bought my first car!

"Yes, I am contented to be here! There's no war. I don't have to be afraid every day. There is always work.

"My daughter, she is so smart. She wants to be a doctor, and she *will* be, because here, she can.

"I haven't seen my mother in twenty years; I can't leave this country, or they won't let me back in. The worst is when I speak to her on the phone. All the time I think, maybe someday I can go home again."

From Mexico:
"I'm doing good now. My children go to school and get what they need. I have a good job. I thank God every day for freedom and a better life, but if it had been me, I would never do what my mama did: I would never leave my children behind and say, I'll send for you.

"My sister and me, we had a lot of family in Mexico. When my mother left, she trusted them to take care of us. Nobody took care of us. We were two girls living alone. My cousin raped me. I never told.

"After I got here, I worked with my mother cleaning houses. We rode buses, sometimes late at night, downtown, very scary. Sometimes we waited a long time to get on and go, and it was hot, so hot, or cold. And on the bus, always someone makes a face, or says something about how we talk, or says, 'There's no room for you, sorry.'

The good thing about speaking another language is, you can pretend you don't understand.

"My mother, she prayed for everyone who had to be downtown at night. All the time she told me, 'God takes care of us. We must be grateful.'

"Because I'm here, I got an education. I got therapy I would never have got, and I stopped being angry.

"I was never far away from my mother again. I was with her when she died.

"For me, I would never go away and leave my children. The care a child needs — you're not going to take away pain with money."

From Mexico:

"After we crossed the border, we walked to Houston for a lot of days. First thing, I found my sister in the taqueria where she worked, and me, so dirty, tired, my legs all scratched, my feet swelled up and full with blisters. I held her a long time. It had been six years since we saw each other. Our parents both dead. Who else did we have? We were so happy.

"I rested one week; then, I went to work. In Estados Unidos, I'll do any work, because here, they pay me."

From El Salvador:
"Three others lived with us in an apartment. In the factory, they paid four dollars and twenty-five cents an hour for twelve-hour shifts. Benefits? Are you joking?"

From Nigeria:
"We were supposed to be one big family reunited back home after we got American diplomas, but none of it happened. My mother and father lost everything. They had to stop sending money. My brothers are still there trying to survive. I stayed on here.

"I live with my aunt and uncle and cousins. We send what money we can. We wait every day for news from home. Every telephone call: who died because they didn't have food, what intellectuals got killed. The family looks to us to keep them alive."

From Mexico:
"After graduation, I jumped into a high-pressure work environment. Then, something changed. Know how I know I've assimilated? I lost that got-to-get-ahead thing. I just don't feel that immigrant desperation any more."

From Argentina:

"I worked in a restaurant — double shifts. One night, I got out around midnight, and my friend gave me a ride as far as Main and West Gray, but I had to walk to Taft to get a bus. I was walking, it was pretty dark, and all of a sudden, three guys came up behind me, and one of them shot me in the back. They didn't steal anything; I think they got scared and ran off.

"I lay in the street until someone came and said, 'Ohmygod, you okay!?' He helped me up. I was able to walk, but I couldn't feel my right arm.

"I got home, and I said, 'I think I'm hurt.' My wife opened my jacket, and she saw blood. She ran to the neighbor, but he said, 'Don't go to the hospital! The *migras* will take you!'

"She found a doctor to come look at it. The bullet had gone clean through.

"I stayed home forty-five days. After that, I promised myself I would learn English so I didn't have to take bad jobs and walk home in the dark, and I would not suffer any more from being an immigrant."

Night after night during my past Hasidic life, as I serenely coached my children through bedtime prayers before our backdrop of God and His law, hungry people were pouring into my city without beginning or end, despite walls and border patrols, often on foot, and I didn't know. They swam the Rio Grande clinging to old inner tubes, or crossed atop trains like riding a beast, or rode packed in airless vans driven by ruthless *coyote* guides or melded into highway commerce crouched behind enormous tires in the undercarriage of eighteen-wheelers trying their best to hold on. Many died. They tumbled between train cars, were shaken from beneath trucks, suffocated in locked vans, drowned in the river. They died in the desert of exposure, snakebite, and thirst. Guides abandoned them without food and water, then robbed or raped and killed them. Others were picked up by the *migras* and sent back, but most of those just turned around and came again.

Those who made it across hid along highways, then walked at night over desert brush dense with guajillo, huisache, agave, all kinds of cacti, and a startling array of venomous snakes, then on through the fertile Texas river valley where it never snows, past miles and miles of citrus, peach, and nectarine groves, and fields of tomatoes, cucumbers, peppers, squash. From Matamoros opposite the southern tip of Texas, the distance to Houston is three hundred fifty-seven miles. One woman I met walked from Matamoros to Houston in high heels.

Thousands more were also relocating to Houston, drawn to international corporations, universities, or family, or plucked from refugee camps by the resettlement organizations that kept major offices in the city. They all came to start over. "This is a city of immigrants," a man from India would tell me. "Everyone you meet here is from somewhere else."

That was beginning to describe most US cities.

Meanwhile, I tucked in another of my children and drew the drapes, trying to seal us off from the world for yet another day.

Scene Two

Binh, *Vien Hoa, Vietnam*

I dreamed I was a child at the seashore, although I was raised an inland kid who didn't know the sea. A salt breeze blew my hair as I dug and dug the sand to the rhythm of crashing waves. The search was on for a coin, a shell, a chunk of gold, a buried civilization. I would dig to China, and there I would find elaborate treasures, vibrant mosaics, all of it ordered and thus comprehensible. The world would be connected then with a clear, true line straight through its murky depths to the light. I would find the hidden line of meaning.

Since the Vietnam War, a generation has passed, and another begun. We have other concerns now. Why delve into this story?

The Vietnam War just might be part of how we became who we are.

The opera company cleared out a storeroom, pulled in an old desk, plugged in a telephone. Many of the people who I had spoken with had referred me on to others; I had accumulated quite a list of names. I took to doing thumbnail interviews from my new office as a screening process. If no one answered, I just moved on down the list; finding Binh was almost random. "I was thirteen when I left Vietnam," the man on the telephone was saying. "I left by accident."

I penciled a star next to his name.

Gangly, alien limbs. Newly thickened hair. Pimples. Suddenly before me were each of my children at thirteen, and my own impatient bid for freedom at that age, while at every step, I still craved my mother's approval. At thirteen, my world, my language, were all *her* — mother and home, home and mother the same. I wanted so badly to grow up and leave her that I couldn't possibly see then how she would shape every step I made away from her.

What if, at thirteen, someone had taken me from my mother and everything I knew? After that, could I know who I was? Or who I might become?

Television sounds and images from my adolescence came back to me: dirt-streaked, barking soldiers; the *whup whup* of helicopters, distant artillery a muted boom; the day's solemn announcement of casualties on the evening news in a polished masculine voice with just the right amount of gravitas. In the years before my withdrawal into Hasidic life, my family rarely missed the evening news and it nearly always included an update on this most documented war in history. Journalists stacked images in the minds of a nation that would never leave us. In one, a naked, malnourished child coated in napalm ran screaming from a burning village, holding her arms like burned sticks out from her body as if she'd been crucified. That photo became proof that an image can stop a war.

Unlike now, US soldiers were conscripted by draft. Service was mandatory, beginning at eighteen, while the right to vote only began at twenty-one; you could die in a war you could not choose. When the president escalated our involvement, the society erupted with protests and screaming draft evaders. There were daily reports of people fleeing into Canada and Mexico.

Our language overflowed with words of rebellion — the language of youth: flower power; ban the bomb; make love not war. Policemen were pigs, anti-establishment a buzzword. Young adults greeted one another with a two-fingered V that stood, not for victory, but for peace.

Violent splinter groups went underground to fight a government that would force them to war. Universities roiled with student marches, demonstrations, sit-ins, building takeovers. There were police showdowns, campus shootings, big public trials, but no one could stop the upheaval, not while men, young and old of every economic class, were being ordered to war.

The generation gap grew fierce, revolution the word of the day. Anyone over thirty represented the corruption that was war. There was a surge of interest in communism and anarchism.

There was a great wave of runaways, running before draft age, or from the draft, or just thrilled with the mystique of freedom in the air. Herds of teens hitchhiked the country. Freedom was everything — born free, to be free, free to be you and me. Middle class families woke to find their son or daughter gone. Young people camped out in public parks where, turned on and tuned out, they took refuge from a broken society. Blissed-out drug use and promiscuity became a panacea. Love is the answer, free love, make love not war. Love was always the answer.

Many fell prey to promises of nirvana. There were roaming gurus, one of them named Charles Manson. Communes popped up across the countryside offering an alternative society where peace, non-violence, equality, and abundant drugs were said to reign.

Blue jeans were a symbol of rebellion, as were leather sandals, long hair, and old t-shirts; anything unwelcome in a job interview was deemed sufficiently anti-establishment. One longhaired friend lived in his blue denim jacket that had an enormous marijuana leaf embroidered across the back and a worn copy of *Quotations of Chairman Mao* ever in the pocket. The jacket smelled as if he slept in it.

We passed around Allen Ginsberg's poem *Howl,* written when we were infants: 'I saw the best minds of my generation destroyed by madness.' Poetry of rebellion was vital, as were music, theater, and dance; they were all essential tools to strip away the artifice of greed that was sending our beloved to die.

We lived on the news. Political awareness was a keen part of our coming-of-age.,
Taught to believe my country was a haven of freedom, raised blind to the segregation around me, I was shocked at the barrage of news images daily exposing our inhumanity abroad. The United States was supposed to be home to justice and fairness. We didn't destroy homes and murder people.

As brothers of friends were being drafted into a horror show, I filled hundreds of pages in my diary with anguished musings about things like US membership in the Southeast Asia Treaty Organization and our questionable responsibility to it.

My sense of identity with a nation began here.

As the war and the Nixon administration began to fail, I found the Hasidim and prepared to run away to my own imagined nirvana.

Thirty years later

His hair was a black brush, his eyes quick and alert. Binh was a short man with a kind face who exuded a doctor-like air of calm competence. He was a practicing chiropractor. We met in the marble-tiled entry of his suburban home, then moved to a sitting area with a high ceiling and accents in red — a pillow, a vase. Although he was younger than I was, I was intrigued with the sense that we had grown up on opposite sides of what the Vietnamese still call 'the American War,' and that we were both marked by it.

A million and a half people of Vietnamese descent lived in the United States because of that war. Houston had the second largest number of Vietnamese Americans in the country.

After polite introductions, we grew silent. Binh's wife wasn't home. He jumped up and insisted on bringing me tea. As we sipped for a moment, I sensed again the paradoxes in this act of listening. There was my need to listen to his silences, to read what I could in his body and face and in the atmosphere of this home. Many had begun by speaking about trying to forget, until we met eyes and they began to remember.

Then, it was as if I woke up. Sitting face to face with a survivor of the Vietnam War finally slammed home for me how different our experiences of that war were. I never saw artillery firsthand or heard neighbors talk about bombed-out homes not far away. I never woke as a child wondering if I was going to die. Our rebellion against American involvement in the Vietnam War was a sort of pretense, a safe substitute for a war we didn't experience, until we believed our rebellion *was* the war. For Americans, the horrors of the Vietnam War were only and ever two-dimensional, a cartoon war on a screen, or reflected like ephemera in the rebellions of others. The American withdrawal was a huge national sigh of relief mixed with shame.

However vivid that era was in memory for us as Americans, however passionate our opposition had been, between Binh and me there was no parity whatsoever to our experiences of war.

And there was this: Binh grew up in South Vietnam, our ally, among people who desperately wanted the Americans to *remain*, then had to deal with the cruel results of our leaving, of our failure.

It would be the same with others I met for this project for whom I knew only secondhand of horrors they may have endured. Once we were face-to-face, my outrage — my so-called trauma — became thin indeed before lived experience.

Here was Binh, his face expectant. I thought, *The people who come to this country fleeing our wars are a gift to us. They are our conscience.*

As to the endless American wars since Vietnam that we fund and drive around the globe, where are those survivors to tell us their stories, with so few of them allowed to get close enough to whisper in our ears?

Binh put down his cup.

"I want you to know that I admire the work you are doing. You are giving people an opportunity to share the memories in their soul that have been waiting inside them for years. It's not just me — there are a lot of stories people like me try to forget because there's too much pain in what they've been through.

"You can't understand how people escaped Vietnam. I mean, a little tiny boat meant for maybe fifteen people with two or three hundred people on top of it. Pretty much a dying experience. So many people died. The women raped. Pirates would take them to an island for their sexual pleasure and keep them prisoner there, didn't feed them, and whoever died just died. A lot of those women who survived later killed themselves. So hard to think about.

Most of us who saw those things, we try to ignore our memories.

"You know, here in the United States, people talk a lot about discrimination, but us Vietnamese, we're way beyond worrying about such things. After what we went through, as long as you don't kill us, we're good. You can see that in the way we don't go out and yell about our rights. No, we find a quiet place and build a little grocery. At least it's ours so we can walk in and feel like nobody's going to try to kill us today.

"Inequality, discrimination — that's just the way people are. We work to survive."

Vietnam was under French colonial rule for over a hundred years until the Vietnamese waged the first Indochina War and expelled the French in 1954. Then, at the Geneva Accords that followed, the victorious rebels lost nearly everything they had gained. This had everything to do with the intervention of Western governments and the machinations of power. As an exercise in divide and conquer, the Accords divided the land the rebels had fought to reclaim into four separate countries, establishing Laos and Cambodia on the inland side, and a long, much-narrowed Vietnam along the South China Sea. They split this new, thinned Vietnam in half across the seventeenth parallel, creating the two separate countries of North Vietnam and South Vietnam. North Vietnam remained communist. South Vietnam established a quasi-democratic government.

North Vietnam went immediately back to war, intent on unifying what was left of their country under communist rule, with China and the USSR. backing them. Ostensibly to stop the spread of communism, the US moved in to support South Vietnam with, incrementally, money, arms, military advisors, air support, and finally, troops, and more troops.

That is, North and South Vietnam became two more pawns in the Cold War. They fought for nearly twenty years. US escalation during that time only galvanized northern communists, who began to call this civil war the "American War." We were the American invaders.

To combat American troops, northern guerillas spread out through the rainforests that blanketed the country, invisible but for tiny flickering lights on nighttime hilltops. They built an elaborate network of tunnels and moved materiel to the front through Laos and Cambodia while US troops remained largely on the surface in an aimless, paranoid march.

American military responded by coating the rainforests with toxic defoliant. They sent snipers into the tunnels, and seeded broad areas with land mines. They sprayed entire villages with napalm — a kind of gelled gasoline — and set the villages on fire. They bombed those transports through Laos and Cambodia (illegally, since the US wasn't at war with either country), and still we couldn't hold the North Vietnamese back. Then, northern forces stormed the gates of the presidential palace in Saigon, capital of South Vietnam and war command center for the South, and the US — we — flew away.

Binh took a breath.

"I was born in 1967 in a little town called Vien Hoa, which is south of Saigon. Since we lived so far south, the war only came to our area in 1975, but we always heard about it. Then, disaster."

Binh had spent his childhood waiting for gunfire that never came. Once the North Vietnamese breeched the presidential palace, the war was over; there was no need to proceed south to Vien Hua. The impact of war and its aftermath came to the area in other ways.

"We were four brothers and an older sister. I'm the youngest. Loi is four years older than me (he used to help my mother in her business), then comes my brother Duc, who was a teacher, and oldest brother Tam, ten years older than me, who was in the army for the South. Then there's my sister, Lan, the oldest. It's a custom in Vietnam that the oldest brother acts like a father for the others. Tam is still like a father to me.

"My father was a soldier for France. When I was five or six, one night he went out with friends, but they came back without him and said he was too drunk to walk. That didn't sound like him. We ran to where he was and got a whole group of guys to carry him home and put him in bed. Next morning, I went to him, and I saw foam around his mouth. I yelled for someone to come, I was crying, but it was too late." He looked solemn. "I was the one who found my father."

I pictured the child Binh was at his father's bedside, his father too still. "Was he a… drinker?" I said. I thought, *Maybe it was a stroke.*

"No, he didn't drink much," Binh said, but he would say nothing more about his father or who they had been together, as father and son.

"It was hard for Mom after he died. Oldest brother Tam was away in the army, and sister Lan married young, and next oldest brother Duc was away at school learning to be a teacher. Only two of us kids were home with Mom — me and my next brother, Loi.

"Mom used to travel to central Vietnam and go into the war zone to buy things to bring home and sell. That was the only way we could get money to buy rice. We'd stay with her sister while she was away. We'd worry so much, but she always came back and brought home stuff to sell.

"You know, now I don't understand how we made it. Whatever we managed to sell at her stand each day brought enough money to buy our food for that day only — usually one liter of rice. It wasn't like we could buy a hundred-pound bag and live on it for months." He laughed. "We lived day to day."

"I may be the youngest, but I helped my mom a lot. Even when I was six, I ran our cigarette stand outside our house by myself. Mom bought cigarettes on loan, then we sold them one at a time, made a little. Most of the time we couldn't get out of debt.

"We ate rice and vegetables. Mom used to tell us how our life was good before the war, but not any more, so we had to mix rice with yam to have enough to eat. That was hard on us. In Vietnam, if you don't have money, you stretch your rice with yam."

Binh's voice dropped.

"Living south of Saigon, we were protected from almost all of the war. I was eight when the North Vietnamese came to Vien Hoa. We didn't know about the surrender. We went outside and saw jeeps and tanks rolling in and bombers overhead, and we thought we were under attack. Everybody ran screaming to the ferries, and we ran, too. There were big crowds trying to get away. When we got near the shore, we saw we had lost our brother Loi."

There was his mother trying to keep the family together in the frenzied crowd, planes overhead, and in the middle of all that, one eight-year-old whose world was coming unglued.

"That was the first time I ever imagined you could get separated from your family and never see them again. I was scared and crying, and I was yelling Loi's name. I looked and looked. Then our Loi just walked up out of the crowd! We ran to him.

"We waited all that night at the ferry dock — me and Loi, and our mom and grandmother and aunt — not even water to drink. Next morning, the ferry came.

"We saw right away that there wasn't room on the ferry for all those people, but people crowded forward anyway. Everyone tried to push through the entrance at once. Shouting and pushing. Someone came out on the deck and tried to manage us by threatening us with a stick. That didn't help.

"I managed to climb up onto the ferry deck. I thought everybody in my family was climbing on after me! I got up thereand turned… and I saw my mom and my grandmother fall under the crowd that was pushing forward. No one stopped to help them; people just stepped on them. I screamed, but no one could hear me. My mother and grandmother were getting crushed. They were going to die.

"Finally, someone pulled them both off to the side and left them on the ground outside the entrance.

"Me, Loi, and my aunt, we said our family is staying together no matter what. We tried to jump off and go to them, but the people in charge pushed us back, and then they locked the entry. They made us wait for hours. Then someone announced, 'There are too many people on this ferry. Some of you have to get off,' and we all jumped off!

"Mom and Grandmother were in pretty bad shape. They were hurt and bleeding. We had to carry them home. For a lot of days, I thought they were both going to die. Me and brother Loi were eight and twelve, but we took good care of them, and they survived."

"Two days later, communist officials made a big official entrance into Vien Hoa. We panicked — two little kids, our mother and grandmother hurt bad, and the enemy coming. We thought the soldiers would say, your family belonged to the South, so we're going to kill you. Then, soldiers knocked on our door. My god, we were scared.

"We opened the door, and they made us go outside and stand in a line beside the street with everybody else in town. We had to wave while the soldiers marched in. Big tanks and trucks rolled by."

Communism had arrived.

"Right away, they said anyone who had been a soldier for the South had to report to them. They said, 'We're just going to interview you a couple of days and then you can go home.' People were afraid not to go for their interviews. My uncle went. Oldest brother Tam had come back from the army, and he went, too. They were both sent to re-education camps — hard labor prisons up north. My uncle didn't come home for five years. Lucky for us, they only kept Tam for a couple of years."

The communists arrested hundreds of thousands of people. They arrested former members of the South Vietnam military, South Vietnamese bureaucrats and politicians, religious leaders, labor leaders, scholars, teachers, lawyers, and any suspected critics of the new regime. Those they arrested were sent to isolated prison camps deep in the northern forests for years of hard labor. It was a life of slow starvation. A staggering number never returned.

"Tam got home from the re-education camp, but since he had been in the army for the South, no one would hire him; he could only get jobs doing menial labor. Officials watched us all the time because of him, and because my uncle had had a high rank in the South Vietnamese army.

"Really, everybody watched everybody. If you had friends over and you served chicken, next day the neighbor asked how you got chicken, and the day after that, police showed up. They walked right into your house and said, 'What were you celebrating?'

"Police gave people points for reporting on each other; the more points you got, the better chance you had of getting a job and food and feeling safe.

"In school, teachers told us, 'Report on your parents so we can teach them how to be good communists.' They said, 'Your parents need to get educated, too, like you. It will be good for them to learn to be good citizens. Report on them for the littlest thing, like wasting paper, or something they did a long time ago.' The teachers made us think, *We want our parents to be like us.* They didn't tell us that if you reported on your parents, officers would come and take your parents away. That happened to some of my friends; they watched police arrest their parents.

"Parents had to be very careful not to talk in front of their kids.

"A few years passed. I helped my mom every day after school. One day, I was working at the cigarette stand, and this man walked up and said, 'Can I buy a cigarette?' I didn't recognize him, and he didn't recognize me. It was my uncle! Normally, 're-education' meant they didn't let you free for ten years or more, but he got out in five years!"

Binh was thirteen.

"My mom came out, and when she saw him, she yelled, 'Oh, my god!' and they... it was so emotional.

"We felt very lucky. Then, we had to tell him that his wife and children left for the United States without him. He couldn't believe it."

"A little before that, in 1979 when I was twelve, the economy was terrible. People were leaving Vietnam for Singapore, Malaysia, Thailand — anywhere they could go. Every day we heard about someone else who escaped the night before, but to get on their boats you had to pay ten ounces of gold for each person, and sometimes more. We didn't have money like that!

"Mom said all the time that she wished we could go, too. She said there was no future for her children in Vietnam.

"Oldest brother Tam still had a hard time getting work. He didn't have money to pay but he really wanted to go. He helped a few different people arrange to leave because he was hoping they might let him on their boat, but those people always got caught by police at the shore. A few other times, people took Tam's money, and then they left without him. Mom got sad every time he failed."

"This is how we ate: the cigarette stand brought in enough to pay for our rice, but also, when people left the country, they left all their things behind. We'd buy that stuff up cheap, wash it up, and then Mom sold it in the flea market. Plus, every day I went out in the woods, and I brought home two big bundles of wood. I was a kid, but I felt that wood was important. I felt I was doing something really important. I felt Mom needed me."

"Duc finished school, and he became a teacher. He got assigned to work in a school in a rural area on a small island, and he had to go live there. He became the principal, but that meant he had the key to the school building. Having the key meant if he ever tried to escape and the police caught him, his punishment would be worse because they would say he failed his responsibility to the country. He'd spend the rest of his life in jail.

"His students understood that, and they also really loved him, so one night, a group of his students got him drunk and took him onto their boat, and they took off with him. Duc left Vietnam for free without even knowing he was going! Really, he's the luckiest of us.

"Everyone used to say, if you get out of Vietnam and you make it to Singapore, that's first-class, and if an American ship picks you up, it's like you won the lottery. Red Cross would give you food and clothes! Then, Duc's boat got picked up by an American ship from Houston, and they took them to Singapore. He sent us a telegram from there. Mom was so happy!

"Mom worried all the time that her kids would get no education and have no future. Every time one of her kids got away it was like the best thing that ever happened to her. It wasn't just her — all the families I knew, if they could get money, they sent their kids out of the country.

"Now Duc was going to be okay, but I could see my mom's secret: Duc's leaving broke her heart. She came home every day and cried a little. I saw how hard it was on her to come home and her son gone.

"After each of my brothers left, in her letters to them she never let them know she was sad, but I knew. No husband, never enough rice, her children disappearing. Without them working, too, she had to beg people. She would say, 'Give me a little — I'll pay you tomorrow.' It got so when they bought her flea market things, they did it just to be kind.

"Some of those customers acted like they were doing a good deed and took our stuff, and then they didn't pay. I used to get so irritated. I would go and sit in front of their house all day until they paid what they owed us. A few of them live in Houston now, and they make fun of me for that. Someone will say, 'You remember him?' and the other will laugh and say, 'How could I forget?' In Vietnam, I might sit outside their house for days until they paid. I felt like, she worked hard, and they took our things and didn't pay?

"Pretty much, I managed collections."

"I used to help my mom make fish sauce. That's a fermented sauce we put on food that was very popular. We made it in twenty-gallon containers. Any time we had a little money, we'd buy fish and add it to the mix. We kept the containers outside so the fish could ferment in the sun, and it became sauce. It was my job to turn it over with a big wooden paddle every day.

"Sometimes I'd say, 'Mom, can I have money?' and she'd say, 'Don't worry, I'm saving up for you. When all the fish sauce is sold, I'll give you a lot.' I never saw any." He laughed. "You know, every batch of fish sauce was like six months of hope. In the US, people buy land. We made fish sauce.

"One time when I was eleven, I took ten or twelve twenty-gallon cans into town by myself. I wanted to show my mom I could do it. A lot of people at the market knew me, and I guess because I was a kid and I was good with words, I sold it all. I brought a lot of money home that day; well, it was a lot to me — I sold cheap because it wasn't in a nice bottle with labels. For our family, it was a lot."

A single twenty-gallon container, at a hundred sixty-seven pounds, would be nearly impossible for the boy to lift. However, Vietnam had adopted the metric system years before this story happened, so Binh might have meant liters and was translating for my American ears.

A twenty-liter container of water weighs forty-four pounds. Sounds more feasible, but a dozen would be five hundred twenty-eight. I didn't ask Binh how an undernourished eleven-year-old moved a dozen such containers to market. I imagined him rallying friends, pictured a gathering of barefoot boys with an assortment of well-used wheelbarrows.

"We had a family boat that was about twelve feet long. One day, me and my brother Loi decided we'd be the men; we'd go fishing and help out our mom — bring in fish to eat and to put in the sauce.

"We went out in our boat. We put the net down; then we weren't big enough to pull it back up. We put the anchor down to try to stay in one place so maybe we could pull up the net, but the water was too deep to put the anchor down there. We lost the net *and* the anchor that day.

"After that, our boat was just something to use for us to have fun and get away from adults for a while. A lot of times, me and Loi would go sleep on it."

"When I was twelve, in school I was top in everything. Then, I won an award, and local communist officials sent me to Saigon for special training to become a future communist candidate. They brought me into an army office. The big important men shook my hand and invited me to sit with them. They said I was the best of Communist Youth. They said I was the future."

Binh looked down and shook his head. "I was even on top in our school's recycling program. Paper was precious; all our paper was brown and hard from recycling it so many times. When we got a piece of paper, we wrote on every inch, front and back. When we came to the United States and went to school, when we saw white, soft, blank paper that you write on one time and throw away, we couldn't believe the luxury."

For the first time, I understood what a shock to the system our throwaway economy, our wealthy disregard of resources, our love of consumables could be for newcomers. I'd never thought that one way to gauge how assimilated someone from Vietnam had become might be to ask, 'Do you still recycle?'

"I taught myself to play guitar. I played outside every night to get people to hang around and buy more cigarettes. I got to know a lot of soldiers because a lot of them would come. They'd stay late, listening and smoking.

"One night, I told a couple of the soldiers about our school's recycling project. Next day, a few of them showed up in military trucks and left load after load of paper at my school, and the school gave me all the credit! I became the leader of the whole recycling program."

Binh looked at his feet like a child betrayed. "You know, that program was just a way to turn us kids into free labor and get us to clean up the town. They wanted to make us feel from the time we were young that we should always give our work to the government for free. We were kids; we didn't understand what they were doing to us.

"My family hated the communists. Every day I went to school excited about school, got awards, and then I came home and my family didn't like what I talked about. They didn't want me to become one of the communists, but I didn't understand that, and they couldn't explain. They knew if they talked against the government even their own kid could get them arrested.

One day my mom and my grandmother sat me down and said, 'We want you to quit school.' I couldn't ask them to explain. You knew what you couldn't talk about. Then, they just pulled me out.

"Loi wasn't doing too well in school, so, after me, he dropped out, too. He's always been a friendly, helpful guy. After that, he always woke up early to do chores. He also helped Mom cook and sell cigarettes. He became like her daughter." Binh laughed. "Me and Loi hung out on our boat a lot, free to do whatever. This went on a few months.

"One night, we were on our boat that was tied up at the dock. There were other kids there — on the shore and also some on their own boats. All of a sudden, one of Loi's friends started yelling, 'Help!' Loi jumped out and ran over to help his friend. Others came over, too.

"The friend asked Loi to help him move a twenty-gallon [or liter] can of oil onto their boat. Sure, he helped — no big deal, but they took a long time doing it. I got bored and went home. I went to sleep.

"Loi, he goes with them down below to put the can down, and suddenly they grab him and hold him while the rest of the family got the boat moving. They escaped Vietnam that night. They said they had to take him with them because he was a witness. If Loi had stayed in Vietnam, and then he talked, their relatives could get hurt.

"I was twelve. I woke up next morning and my brother was gone."

"Was that happening a lot?" I said.

"A whole lot of people were leaving."

"Suddenly like that?"

"Yes."

"This time was different, though. It was your brother. Your best friend," I said.

"Exactly.

"Usually, a whole family disappeared together. The next day, everybody would figure out which family was gone, and within one day there'd be nothing left of their house. People took the tin roof, the walls, the poles that held it up.

"That day, we went outside to see which house was gone, and then we knew who took our Loi.

"Now two of us had left Vietnam. Neither of them even planned to go, and our mom didn't have to pay for it!"

He smiled.

"Always, every time my mom heard another family had left, she got sad and said she wished her son could go with them and make it out of Vietnam. Now that Loi was gone, Mom said she was happy, but my god, I worried about Loi. We'd heard about many boats that went the wrong way and got lost, and anyway those boats weren't meant to go out on the ocean. Most of the time, a wave went over and washed everybody overboard.

"We didn't know if Loi was alive or dead. My mother and I both worried, but we didn't share it. She said she was happy, but I saw she had pain in her heart.

For three months, she slept, but she didn't. She ate, but not really. I saw her, but it wasn't her. She worked; then she walked home with our bag of rice for that day with her eyes on the ground. I walked with her, but she didn't talk, except she kept saying, 'One of these days, you will also go to America.'

"I would say, 'Okay, Mom,' but all I knew was, I lost my brother and Mom needs me more now. She didn't even know where America was. I didn't either. I wasn't ever going to leave her.

"Then, we got a telegram. Loi was in Malaysia."

The previous year, in June of 1978, the first group of Vietnamese refugees arrived by boat at Bidong Island, a previously uninhabited island in the South China Sea off the coast of Malaysia. They waded ashore, gathered brush for fire, built shelters, fished, and foraged for food. Soon, another boat showed up, and another.

The Malaysian Government moved quickly to build a refugee camp on Bidong. Seven months after the first group, that camp was the most densely populated place in the world, with more than forty-thousand people crowded into an area the size of a football field. Loi had sent the telegram from Bidong Refugee Camp. A quarter of a million people would eventually pass through there.

In 2005, despite vehement protests by residents, the Malaysian Government forced the last nine thousand people of Bidong to return to Vietnam. They fought the return to their home country, despite the difficult life in the camp and their many years of waiting to get to freedom.

Today, the empty camp is a tourist attraction. You buy a ticket; there are docents, and tours.

"Loi's boat was crowded, but everyone survived. Oh, we were happy when we heard.

"My mom — I never saw a woman pray from gratitude so much in my life. Going to church wasn't enough. She went outside and prayed to the sky, to my dad, my grandparents, to all the ancestors. Catholic, Buddhist — if there was a saint anywhere, she called the name and said, 'Thank you! Take care of him.'

"The truth is, Loi had a rough time in the camp, but he never let her know. Instead, he wrote, 'They're treating me like a king here. I drive a car. I pick apples from the side of the road.' All lies.

"Mom was so happy! She kept saying, 'You see your brothers? You'll have that, too. Keep praying, and I will work hard.' I thought, *I'm all she has left, and she wants me to leave?*

"You know, before then, when we got the first telegram from Duc saying he made it to Singapore? She heard 'Singapore' like her son just got into Harvard." We both smiled.

Then, he sighed. "Mom said my sister Lan was so good in business she could do okay under any government. She said Lan would be okay whether she stayed in Vietnam or left.

"She worried most about oldest brother Tam, who was still in Vietnam, because he couldn't get work. I thought Tam would be next to leave, so imagine my surprise when one night Mom woke me up in the middle of the night, hugged me and kissed me, and said, 'It's your turn. I saved the money for you. I'm so happy! Now, you go too.'

"I sat up and… tears. Why was she sending me away? Someone I didn't know came into the room, and Mom said I had to go with him. I couldn't ask. I couldn't refuse, but when I left, my heart was broken. I couldn't understand why I had to go.

"The man took me to a house, and he locked me in a little room. I sat alone for three days and couldn't talk to anybody. Then, they just opened the door and sent me home. It was a scam to take Mom's money.

"I ran home. Mom hugged me and cried real hard, but she never did explain.

"After that, I figured she had lost the money to send me, and she had nothing left to pay anyone else to take me away. I was happy."

"Were things at home the same after that?"

"Oh, yes. I jumped right back into normal life."

I thought, *Normal.*

With two brothers gone, Binh worked even harder to help his mother. He played guitar near the cigarette stand every night. He saved all the bits of money he could and used it to buy small useful items, then hid them for his mother to sell in an emergency. He thought of his hidden collection as a home savings account, for her security.

It must have been during this time that Binh bought himself a *num ti*, which means 'half an ounce' — a stamped ring made of a half-ounce of twenty-four carat gold. Those rings were regarded as a bank on your finger and a common way to store savings. Once Binh had the *num ti*, he never took it off.

From 1955 until 1975, in what was still the Republic of Vietnam, a company called Kim-Thanh manufactured and sold 'portable gold' or *mot luong* — a stack of rectangular leaves of gold foil wrapped in printed oil paper that weighed about a gram. Each leaf of gold was embossed in French and Vietnamese. As the communists advanced in 1975, people sold their belongings and put their money into these *mot luong*, often sewing the leaves into their clothing. Most of the people who left by boat bought their way aboard with these packets, ensuring the refugee boats would be plum targets for pirates.

"I often stayed out all night at the shore. All the kids of our town did that. We'd hang around the dock or on the bridge above it, me playing guitar. Part of it was the way all the adults in charge were always snooping on us, watching us, and watching each other. We couldn't get away from them. Adults in the Communist Party or in school or in the neighborhood were constantly around us, and there were secrets everywhere we weren't allowed to speak; everyone watched you and knew everything about you and told on you, and you couldn't talk about it. Out on the dock at night we could get away and relax.

"We'd stay out all night. It got so dark you could hardly see, but the bridge would be packed with kids. When the sun came up, the boys would strip off their shirts, grab a rope that hung from the bridge, and jump in the water. We'd swim around, then climb back up the rope.

"Nearly every family had a fishing boat; there were a lot of boats parked around that dock. Sometimes at night, we'd see someone trying to leave. I think about it now — if a boat started pulling out, we'd all start yelling for fun, even though we were making it really dangerous for them. We thought it was exciting.

"This one night, some of us jumped onto one of the boats because we thought their boat was so big. It was just play — we got on, then off, then back on, the rest of our friends sitting around on the bridge.

"Then, we quit and went and joined them on the bridge. The sun was coming up. Some of us started leaving for home.

"Suddenly, a group of people carrying bags and packages showed up and started boarding the boat we'd been playing on. They were being very quiet, and that told us they were probably planning on going somewhere, maybe for good. Also, their boat wasn't tied down, but a lot of people did that.

"From up on the bridge, we saw their bags and thought, *Food*. One guy said, 'Maybe we can get breakfast!' We were hungry. He asked me to go with him.

"The two of us went and followed those people onto their boat. A bunch of the other kids followed, too — there were fifteen of us in all. I started talking to a guy who looked like he might be the owner. 'Hi. What's your name? Got any food?' And then, the motor started. The boat started to move.

"At first, I thought, *No big deal*. Then, the man I'd been talking with yelled, 'Get down!'

"Everybody fell to the floor. No one spoke. Then, I saw we were passing a police station, so I thought, *Oh, normal, hiding from police.*"
Right around this time, the US established the Orderly Departure Program, which offered Vietnamese people legal, safe, free transport to the United States — if they qualified. The program would reduce the number leaving by boat, but not stop them.

"At the mouth of the harbor, mountains stuck out into the water on either side. Nobody ever took a fishing boat past the mountains. That just didn't make sense — the ocean floor dropped real deep right there, and the waves got big. Then, we were passing the mountains. Some of the kids started to freak out.

"Suddenly, up comes another boat and stops alongside ours, and fifteen or so more kids got on with us! About half of those kids were as young as me, and the rest were older. Then, that boat sped away.

"You see, this was a planned rendezvous. This new group of kids, they were relatives of the boat owner and also kids of his close friends. Their parents had been planning to come, too. The boat owner had told the parents to send their kids ahead so they might make it to freedom even if the parents got caught. He planned to pick up all the parents at a second location.

"The guy who brought those kids must have also brought news, because shortly after, the boat owner came out and told us, 'I just got word that the rest of my family and crew were caught by police, and the police are now looking for us. We're not going back. We're family now, and we're going to America. If we die, we die together.'

"It was November eighteenth, 1980. I was thirteen. I had no shoes."

"We were thirty kids plus the boat owner, his wife, and daughter. They had planned to collect two hundred fifty more adults at the other location.

"We went below to the bunks and got in. My mom always told me I'm going to America, but I never thought it was real. In the quiet, the realization kicked in, for all of us. *You're not going to see your parents any more. Forever.* The boat was rocking; nothing solid under us. One guy cried. Then another. It was like a momentum. You can hear the opera."

I asked Binh if he had ever told anyone this story before. He closed his eyes and shook his head.

"The hardest part came later when the boat owner came back to tell us they didn't have food for all of us. One of the older boys asked him where we were going, and the boat owner just said, 'north.' We could tell he didn't really know where.

"No food and no directions, and we were moving out to sea.

"You've seen the movie *The Perfect Storm?* That was us. When a wave hits, the boat goes up high. When it comes back down, you're in freefall starting from so high you're sure no one is going to make it, you'll break every bone, but then the boat is going up again, even higher this time. Every wave, you hang on like you never knew you could, then you fall and you're sure you can't do it even one more time. So much pain, you stop feeling. You scream and scream. Everything runs out of you, snot, vomit, shit all over you. You are thrown to the floor.

"I was sure I was going to die. I wanted it to be over."

"We had two days hard like that. During a break in the storm, the boat owner came down and told us, 'Pray. Pray to your mom, your dad, your grandparents, whoever you can ask to help us.'

"I prayed. I prayed to my mother, to Virgin Mary, to Jesus. I said, 'Help us. Oh, God, please help us.' Then the storm started up again."

He prayed to his mother. Binh really was just thirteen, his mother still his goddess. He was sure he couldn't live without her, or she without him.

Then it seems Binh fell asleep...

"Early the third day, I opened my eyes, and something was different. It was quiet outside. Water was lapping the sides. The boat was rocking.

"One by one, we stood up. We climbed the ladder up to the deck and stood around up kind of dazed.

"The water was smooth like you could put a plate on it. I sat down against a wall and pulled up my knees. I stayed there all day. It was quiet, but that wasn't so good. In the quiet, I went through all the people I loved, one by one, and I cried a long time. Then... I just stopped. I got calm. It was like I understood what I had to do; I had to save every bit of myself for the job of surviving one more day or one more hour. There was no more time for crying. I just wondered, *What will it feel like in the water? How does it feel when you die?*

"I became a different person. You see?"

"One of the older boys took charge — we knew the adults didn't know where we were going. Every hour, he sent another one of us up the mast to look for ships, even after dark. He also looked around the boat and found cans of condensed milk and a few cans of water. He punched a hole in one at a time and passed it around. He told everyone they could take one sip.

"The boat owner told us to look around for something like a stick we could use because there were Thai pirates in the area. He said, 'Those pirates will try to kill you.' He said we'd have to fight for our lives.

"Nothing surprised me anymore. Nothing scared me anymore. I would hold my stick and hope. If I had to, I could be a man for a minute.

"Very soon, we saw two boats coming straight at us, fast. The owner's wife and his daughter ran below to hide in the bunk and one of us followed to cover them up — to not let the pirates know we had females aboard.

"Then, the boats came alongside ours, and we saw the Thai writing on the side. When they stopped, all they saw was a bunch of skinny boys sitting in a row, not talking, looking straight ahead. I had my hand with the ring on it tucked under my leg. Nobody moved. Nobody made a sound.

"Maybe someone had tipped them off, and they had been looking for us. Maybe they expected our boat to have more than two hundred adults on it like it was supposed to, and they expected most of them had paid in *num ti* gold bars or packets of gold, but all they saw was us boys, bare feet, bare arms, bare chests. They looked at each other, and took off.

"We could breathe again."

"Another day, we saw a big ship. It was so big, we were sure it was American. We were so happy! They'd take us to America. Everything would be good!

"We got up close. We were rocking from the big waves their ship made. Then, we saw that the boat was Russian, and their captain started yelling into a microphone, 'Go. Go!'

"We heard him like he was saying, 'Get out of our way! Get out of here!' Now I wonder, maybe he was warning us about something. Pirates? Or that they were going to start shooting?

"Anyway, they weren't going to help us. We turned and sped away. We were just relieved we didn't get killed.

"We kept moving through the next day and the next, but it seemed like we were going nowhere. We could only see water in every direction. We passed around the last can of condensed milk.

"By the next day, we were so weak we didn't care about anything. We lay sprawled all over the deck not even trying to protect ourselves from the hot sun any more. Then my mother was touching my face with a soft, soft touch. I looked up into her eyes. I looked across the deck, and I saw my brother Loi running away. I wanted to chase after him, but I couldn't get up; I couldn't follow. I called him and called him. I was thinking I had to run after Loi and be careful not to trip over the kids all over the deck, but other voices were crying, and… this pain in my side. I kept trying to call out to Loi.

"The sun went down, and maybe from sea mist, I woke up. Other boys woke up, too. Most of us were too weak to stand. A ship was approaching!

"Our boat owner got on the radio to talk with them. For two hours, he begged them to take us onto their ship and save us. He said he'd leave his boat behind if they'd take us on.

"We dozed and waited. I was starting not to care.

"Their captain refused.

All of a sudden, a ladder unrolled down the side of their ship, and six men came down it. One of them brought down a can of concentrated oil. The others were carrying one end of a long flexible tube that was attached to their deck. The tube was wide enough for a person to crawl through it.

"They checked our motor and added oil. Someone on their deck dropped a water hose down through the tube and turned on the water. Their guys sprayed all the vomit and diarrhea off our bunks. They sprayed down the floors and deck. They sprayed us. The water was hard, but we put our faces in, and we rubbed our hands in it. We tried to catch it and drink it.

"Someone on their ship dropped down packages that held sheets of folded plastic. The men opened the sheets and spread them over the bunks. They also dropped down cans of food, bottles of water, and packets of Kool-Aid."

Kool-Aid is an icon of American childhood. The brand name was so utterly out of context in the South China Sea that hearing it jerked me back to the present, and then on to memories of drinking water flavored with that ubiquitous sweetened powder. "Did you even know what Kool-Aid was?" I said.

"No! Those little packets? We had no idea what you're supposed to do with them! We licked the powder straight out of the paper.

"You know, I came across that stuff in the grocery store in Houston years later, and I couldn't believe it when I saw it! Then, I read the back.

That's when I first learned we were supposed to mix it into pitchers of fresh water. What we would have done for pitchers of fresh water! I just stood there and shook my head."

Here's adult Binh on his way home. He stops in some brightly lit Houston supermarket for eggs and orange juice. He's pushing a grocery cart. He's finished college and is now in chiropractic school, his head full of anatomy lessons, or he's older and married, his practice well established, in a white coat with his name embroidered in black above the pocket. He passes an aisle cap display of Kool-Aid…and suddenly he's a barefoot boy on an open boat, the stench and rocking, hunger and heat. A kid waiting calmly to die. *'I was thirteen. I had no shoes.'*

"Maybe we were giving up, but we were just happy to get our first food in three days, and happy they left us enough food and water to make it three or four more days. It was enough that life kicked in a little. We weren't even disappointed that they didn't let us on their ship.

"We made the food last five days. Then, we were out of food again. This time we got really sick. We had some water left, but we started vomiting, and more diarrhea, and the waves were bad. I lay on my bunk certain I was going to die. I just wanted it to be over. Once or twice, I crawled up to the deck and tied myself to a pole for fresh air that didn't stink.

"Somehow, I don't know how, nearly all of us managed to take our turn up on the mast.

"On the seventh day at about six in the morning, I had just finished my watch and come down. One of the boys had just replaced me. I was headed below hoping to get a drink when I heard someone yelling, 'An island! There's an island!' I ran back up to the deck.

"It was the most beautiful place I'd ever seen. There were palm trees with coconuts. Everything was green.

"The boat owner stopped the boat near the shore. He said, 'There's no one here. We can rest. Pull off your clothes, jump in, and wash yourselves. I'll throw your clothes down — scrub them, too.'

"We stripped and jumped in. The water was shallow and warm. We went under, rubbed our heads, and tried to get clean. Soon, we started to feel better. We laughed and splashed each other. Maybe we were going to make it after all.

"We were still playing and splashing when two motorboats filled with men in uniforms came roaring up. We freaked out, us naked in the water and them pointing guns at us and hollering. We scrambled back onto our boat. A group of soldiers came on after us. We thought, *This is it.* There we were, again in a row, a bunch of skinny kids afraid to move, men eyeing us who just might kill us.

"Who were they?" I said. "What country were they from?"

"We never figured that out.

"We sat half a day while they searched every inch of our boat. They stole anything they wanted. They took all our watches and jeans. Most of our clothes were ragged and wet, and they left those alone."

Once again, a wide-eyed row of skinny boys sat so tightly together that not one of the men noticed the one with his hand shoved beneath his thigh; on his finger, a gold ring.

"Then another military boat showed up. They tied a rope to ours and pulled us to another part of the shore. They made us get into our clothes and get off the boat.

"We stood on the shore and watched them pull our boat away. They even stole that. Behind us, there was nothing but trees and a path that was red dirt."

The path led through overgrowth to a house where a woman was working her garden. I picture her in a conical hat bent over, a basket over her arm. She took one look at the emaciated group and understood that they had come across the ocean. It is quite possible they were not the first. She gestured, 'Come with me.'

It was a short walk down the path to the cluster of tin shacks with thatched roofs that constituted a village. She herded the group into a small yard and closed the gate, then disappeared into the house.

Soon, a man came out. He picked up a garden hose and began to spray the group. Binh and the others pulled in close to one another and put their palms up against the rushing water, but they were too ashamed to object or step away. "We were horrified. The yard made me think of a pigpen, and that meant we were animals. He sprayed us like we had a disease."

Binh didn't notice how different his reaction was compared to the day that unknown sailors boarded their boat at sea and sprayed them down with a hose, but those sailors did so as a kindness, and helped them to get clean when they couldn't do so. Now, the boys had just washed themselves in the bay. Besides, this man could have ushered them inside his house and offered them showers, soap, and towels, instead of spraying them in a yard.

"I thought we couldn't go lower than this. Where were we? What were they going to do to us? Then I realized, *These are good people. They want to help.*"

Binh had just been snatched from a country and a childhood in which everyone betrayed everyone. He had been tricked into leaving his home, threatened by pirates, chased by Russians, abandoned by Americans, robbed by police, then sprayed like… a pig. "How did you trust that they were good people?" I said. *How could you trust anyone?*

"I didn't at first, but then, I just knew."

I thought, *Maybe he saw a smile, heard a kind voice. Maybe to this boy, it was all like food.*

Someone came and led them, dripping, into a nearby building where they crouched on the floor to wait and wonder. After a while, a woman arrived and brought others bearing trays of hot grilled fish and rice.

The group was incredulous when they saw the food. They pointed at one another like a question, *Is this for us??* and they pointed at the sheer quantity — the impossibility of it. They laughed as the women handed out chopsticks. Presuming no one in the village had that many bowls, they took the chopsticks and ate off the platters.

"We ate and ate. The women kept pointing at the food and smiling as if to say, take more. And finally, we smiled too. Not one of us had died. That's unusual for boat people.

"That was the happiest day of my life."

It is said that more than a third of the two million people who fled Vietnam, Cambodia, and Laos by boat in those years died at sea. They died from storms, heat, thirst, starvation, they were washed overboard, of wounds that festered, or their hearts failed, or they were raped or robbed and then killed by pirates. The survivors ended up in refugee camps in Malaysia, Thailand, and Singapore.

"I slept on the floor most of that day. When I woke up, it was almost dark. I heard helicopters outside."

Binh sat up. Some of the boys were standing around in the dim light. Binh stumbled outside, rubbing his eyes.

"I thought maybe the helicopters were from the UN or some related organization; I wasn't sure who sent them, but to us, they looked American, and because of that, we were happy. They took us by helicopter to Tanjung Pinang, in Indonesia."

Tanjung Pinang is the capital of the Riau Islands, an old Malay port city at the southern end of Bintan Island with quick ferry connection to Singapore. It sounded like their boat had landed on or near Bintan Island. The American Red Cross maintained an office in a Tanjung Pinang hotel as a base from which to address the Vietnamese refugee crisis.

From Binh's village of Vien Hoa to Bintan Island, the distance is over three-thousand miles.

"They put us in a classy hotel and let us bathe. They gave us hygiene packets… and new clean clothes… and a clean bed."

Binh left a dramatic pause between each item in this list of riches. His voice was full of a boy's excited wonder.

Days of adequate food, water, shelter, and healing sleep passed in a blur. During that time, Red Cross employees called each member of the group into an office for a medical exam and a detailed interview. When Binh's turn came, he found the man in a white coat patient and kind. Binh gave him his mother's name and address in Vietnam. He named his sister and brother who were also in Vietnam, then added that his brother Duc was in a refugee camp in Singapore and Loi was in another in Malaysia. He mentioned his aunt and uncle in America by name and said he didn't know exactly where they were. The man asked many questions about Duc and Loi.

"That night after I talked about my family, I lay awake in the dark a long time. My stomach was full, and I was clean and comfortable, but that meant I could feel something again. All night, I missed my mom. Who was going to get the wood for her now?"

There was a local man who spoke Vietnamese who often went to that Red Cross hotel to meet new arrivals. People called him 'Papa' and referred to him as an angel. The man gave Binh paper and pencil and told him to write a letter to his mother.

"I wrote my mother everything that happened to me. I told her about the storm and the pirates and the island. I told her that I was safe now, and that the Red Cross was taking care of me, and I made sure to tell her where all the stuff was that I hid for her. I said she should sell it so she could take care of herself."

The man mailed Binh's letter to his mother. He also contacted someone he knew in South Vietnam and asked his friend to find Binh's mother and tell her in person that the boy was alive and well.

"Years later, my sister told me that my mother was just as devastated after I left as she was when my brothers left, and this time she didn't hide it, until she got my letter. The letter gave her hope."

"We stayed in the hotel for ten days. Then the Red Cross took us to Galang Refugee Camp. I had new shorts and a shirt, but still no shoes."

Galang Refugee Camp was on Galang Island, another of the Riau Islands of Indonesia and a short trip from the Tanjung Pinang hotel straight across part of the South China Sea. From 1979 until 1996, when the Galang refugee camp closed, more than a quarter of a million people passed through. The vast majority were Vietnamese, the rest from Cambodia and Laos. All of them were displaced by the Vietnam War and by the extreme regimes that formed in war's aftermath. In the void.

"I walked up to the barbed wire fence at the front of the camp. It's strange remembering this now — it seems like I walked up by myself even though I know there was a whole group of us. I figured word had gone around that a new group had arrived because there were lots of people at the fence who had come to see us. They looked excited and happy. People stuck their hands through the fence and waved and yelled to get our attention."

Then it was as if adult Binh became the boy he was that day at the fence, as if it was all happening just now. We were together at the fence. His face was troubled, quizzical. "They yelled 'Where are you from?' They called out the names of their towns and of their husbands and wives and brother and sisters — so many names I couldn't make out most of them because they were all yelling at once, but it felt like their voices were very far away. I couldn't move. I felt lost."

Binh was dissociating. He seems to have remained in this isolated state of mind. From this point, he continued to speak as if he had been alone; he did not mention the people who had been with him on the boat again, except to note when they left.

"Inside the camp, someone directed me to Central Barrack. I walked in and stood at the back, too scared to do anything. I watched some people find one other. They were hugging and laughing. I started to cry.

"Someone took pity and came over and told me to go take a number. I did, but I didn't get in line or talk to anyone. I just stood there and tried not to cry. Then, someone else called to me from across the room and said, 'You! You have to go to Orphan House.'

Binh's voice broke. "He called me 'orphan.'" Just then, a man dressed as a clown walked into Central Barrack. Like the 'angel' of Tanjung Pinang, the man was himself a refugee. He used to dress like a clown and go into Central Barrack every day looking for newcomers; he would walk through the camp and try to cheer people up.

Binh said that today the man is a comedian in California. He said Vietnamese Americans love him for what he did back then.

"The clown got down in front of me and said, 'Why are you crying? Don't cry! You're free!' He looked all around and said, 'Where are your parents?'

"I didn't talk.

"He put a hand on my shoulder and said, 'You have a brother or sister?'

"I hiccupped that one brother was in Singapore.

"He said, 'Wait — some people from Singapore just came! Come with me.'

"We walked through the camp looking for my brother, but we just seemed to be wandering among thousands of people. Finally, he said, 'Promise me you won't give up. Ask everyone you see. Someone will know your brother,' and he left me there."

Camp One was for new arrivals waiting to be approved for resettlement. Once approved, residents were moved to Camp Two, where they could enroll in classes to study various languages and even get lessons in western culture.

Here's a dazed and shoeless boy in a new shirt, a ring on his finger, on his first day in a refugee camp wandering alone among tens of thousands of people. His mouth is dry, his stomach empty. He gives up and sits down on the ground to watch passersby. He becomes a speck that no one notices. The boy is bewildered. His mind is shutting down.

Binh sat there for some time. Then, he remembered his promise to a clown. He sighed, and got up.

I assume the clown had led their fruitless search for newcomers from Singapore through

Camp One. Later I would understand that, once he was alone, Binh must have wandered into Camp Two.

After a few aimless minutes, Binh glanced in the open doorway of a random barrack. Inside, people were talking to one another in Vietnamese. He turned away, but one of the voices... Binh turned back and took a step into the barrack. There was someone talking, someone he couldn't see in a hammock pulled high. He furrowed his brow and half whispered a name as an impossible question: 'Duc?'

Duc was the next oldest brother whose students got him drunk and took him from Vietnam. He had been moved here from Singapore.

"Duc rolled out of the hammock and dropped to the ground. Yelling my name, he ran up and wrapped his arms around me and held me tight. I kept saying, 'Duc, Duc, Duc.' He held me a long time.

"All of a sudden, he pushed me away and ran outside yelling, 'Mom! Mom?' He couldn't imagine I could have come alone."

Binh stayed inside and waited for Duc to realize.
. "Duc ran back in and said, 'Where are they? Who's with you?' He sounded like a wild man.

"I said, 'I'm by myself.'

"Duc broke down then. He cryied and said, 'My god, my god.'"

"Finally, I was happy again. I told Duc everything that happened to me, and I showed him my *num ti*."

"Duc took me to Orphan House, and he told the person in charge, 'This is my brother. He is not an orphan. He's staying with me.'

"Next day, he took me to this place where you could sell your gold so you could buy what you needed in the camp. A guy there at a table weighed my ring on his scales. Then he cut the ring in half and gave me the value of half of it in coins, plus a piece of stamped gold equal to the other half. The first thing I did was buy cigarettes for Duc. Then I bought shoes."

Food was given out once a week. The food mainly consisted of dried beans and rice that residents cooked on open fires. The allotment wasn't nearly enough to last the week. This fact drove a busy camp economy. This is true of refugee camps the world over.

"The camp was like a country of its own. Lots of people had stands and sold things. There were also different offices — from the UN and the Red Cross and other organizations — that were there doing things to help us. There were also schools where you could study different things, like English. Duc said I had to go and learn."

This, then, was Camp Two, where such services were offered. Duc must have been approved for resettlement before Binh arrived.

"I wanted to go to work, but Duc insisted I had to learn English. I went to school every morning. I also found work at a stand that sold pots and pans and went there every day after school. Also, just like Mom did in Vietnam, I collected stuff from people who left for America that they left behind, and I sold it.

"When I got better at English, I quit school and started working all day. I didn't tell Duc, but since sometimes I bought him the very best cigarettes, he started getting suspicious. He went and found out what I was doing. Then… I hired him!

"We became big shots. We always had plenty of rice, and we even had a rainwater container. In the camp, to have your own rainwater container was a very big deal."

The weather never varies on Bintan: Fahrenheit Mid-eighties by day, mid-seventies at night, with an average yearly rainfall of ninety-six inches — nearly double the annual rainfall in subtropical, flood-prone Houston. With no plumbed water in the camp, a rainwater container was a valuable item.

"Duc canceled his application to go to the United States and started a new joint application. He wanted to make sure that we left together and that we went to the same place. That put him back at the end of the line. We would wait together.

"One by one, all the kids who had been on my boat were processed and left, including the boat owner and his wife and daughter. I never saw any of them again."

"Seven months passed. Duc and I worked hard and tried not to think about time passing. At night, we talked about our plans. Every day, we went to the Red Cross office and asked them to find Loi, and reminded them that we had an uncle in the USA.

"Meanwhile, back in Vietnam, the communists must have decided that oldest brother Tam was rehabilitated because, even though he'd been a soldier for South Vietnam, they gave him *and* my sister Lan jobs in the government!

"Tam's coworkers knew he wanted to leave the country. They also knew he wouldn't dare try to go because he would never jeopardize our mother. Then, some of Tam's police friends organized it. Really, it's true! Police put Tam, his wife and children, my sister Lan and her husband and children, plus my uncle who had gotten out of jail, into a police boat and took them out in the water as far as the border.

"My mother refused to go with them. She said she had to take care of her mother, and my grandmother wasn't strong enough to go.

"At the last minute, Lan's husband was overcome with fondness for Vietnam. He said, 'I can't. Maybe later, but I can't;' then he jumped into the water and swam back to shore."

"Duc and I had been in the camp thirteen months when, one morning, we heard our names on the loudspeaker calling us to the office. It was time to leave for America!

"We talked a lot that night trying to decide what to do about Loi. We knew he was in a refugee camp in Malaysia, and even though we wanted very much to go to America, and we didn't want to lose our chance, we didn't want to go without him. If we didn't all go together, we were afraid we'd lose one another, maybe forever. We wanted the Red Cross to find Loi and bring him to us. That seemed to be the only way we could all leave together.

"We decided we would pass up our chance to go to America if we had to. No matter what, we'd wait for our brother.

"One day, someone came and told us they heard on the camp radio that Tam and Lan and my uncle had arrived with their families. We were sure our mother was with them. Oh, how we ran! I was laughing and running like my heart would burst."

Hearts full, hands on their shoulders as if to make sure they were real, happy cries. *Are you really here?* It all seemed like a doughnut of sweetness with a hole in the middle. Binh did not speak of discovering that his mother had not come. Maybe he could not.

"Tam and Lan were now with us in the camp. It would take months until they got processed. We decided they could wait for Loi, instead of us. Duc and I would go on to America. I sold the other half of my ring and bought us good jeans and shirts.

"I wrote out a will and hung it outside the place where we slept and where we kept our pots to make our food and all the things we had for trading. I wrote: 'These things inside here belong to my family who is coming very soon. Please save all of it for them'."

I didn't understand why carrying their goods over to Tam and Lan in Camp One was not an option. I didn't ask.

"Duc and I left the next day. We heard later that the minute we left, residents came and took everything."

Binh stopped talking. It felt like the end of an era.

"Had you ever been on an airplane before?" I asked.

"No," he said.

There was the shudder and roar of takeoff, that first time rising above the clouds. My first flight in my life took me away from the world as I knew it and into Hasidic life. Binh's first flight would be just another step into adulthood descended on him too soon.

In Houston, the brothers found their way to baggage claim, past signs in English that Binh couldn't translate despite his studies in the camp, then outside into the steaming air. They settled on a bench to wait. No one came for quite a while. Then a stranger walked up and spoke to them in Vietnamese.

"Duc jumped up like he knew the man. Then I saw that he resembled our mom. He was our uncle!

"I was very happy. I wanted to leave right away for our new home, but my uncle was smiling like he had a secret. He said, 'Wait. There's another flight coming.' Then, out came Loi! His hair had grown very long, and he was carrying a little bag. Red Cross had found us, found him, found our uncle, and put us all together!"

Like marbles tossed across a map.

"We had not seen one other for two years. Me and Loi and Duc laughed and jumped on each other. It was like the Fourth of July."

A new kind of Independence Day.

When it was over, when Binh was done, we looked at each other. He stood up and asked me to follow.

Back when Binh was a new doctor planning to marry, his mother sent him a *mot luong* packet of gold leaves to pay for his wedding. She had worked and saved for years to be able to buy it for this purpose.

Binh led me to a back room to a small, draped table, on it, a shrine to his mother — one framed photograph of an unsmiling woman with a direct gaze and shoulders squared at the center, before it, a rice bowl, a pair of chopsticks, and the *mot luong* that had been her gift. "She died alone in Vietnam," Binh said. There was resignation in his middle-aged face, and the need for a mother that never goes away.

I pointed to the packet, "May I ask? What was it worth at the time that your mother sent it?"

"About twelve dollars."

The room had wall-to-wall carpeting, drapes over the window, decorative pillows on a freshly made bed, pictures neatly arranged on the wall. It was a perfect picture of middle-class American suburbia. "I'm forty years old," Binh said, "but inside of me, I'm still a kid. We don't have children, but some day, I want to go back to Vietnam and adopt an orphan."

I stepped out of Binh's home that day into a world that seemed forever changed. Walking to my car, I thought of the wars we were raging in Iraq and Afghanistan, and our ongoing drone strikes in the Middle East and Africa, our endless wars.

We no longer hear foreign place names like My Lai and Hue and Hanoi night after night in our living rooms until they settle familiar on our tongues, nor do we hear reports of current battles, or of the number of people killed, announcements that once made us close our eyes and see red pooled on the ground. We've forgotten the sound of the *whup whup* of a helicopter or the specific distant rumble of artillery, and we see no photographs of burned children running away. No one gets drafted into the military anymore either, so there are few large public protests about war, and no mobs of rebellious youth. From the distance of time, it seems that in some ways, we opposed American involvement in the Vietnam War because we felt it was our right to remain safely in our cocoon. No one told us back then to be careful what we asked for.

Now our wars are without image or sound, and very few survivors are allowed close enough to whisper their stories in our ears.

At the Vietnam War Memorial, Washington DC:
The march of disembodied names etched into black granite was as ordered as troops across a blackened landscape. Notes and letters and flowers, plastic and real, were taped to some of the names, wreaths and vases at my feet on the walkway beneath others. I paced through the memorial to a muttered aleatory of death.

I became Binh, an American man looking at etched walls that would never include the name of a single Vietnamese ally who died in battle or in a Vietnamese prison, or the name of any of the Vietnamese who died by US bullets, bombs, napalm, poisons, or land mines, but then, if these walls named all of the dead from the Vietnam War and not just fifty-eight thousand US soldiers; if it also named civilian dead, and listed them from both sides of that war; if it added those left maimed, burned, raped, blinded, sickened, mad, orphaned, homeless, rootless, addicted, suicidal, haunted, poverty-stricken, unable to work, robbed of their history, and unable to have dreams beyond survival; if it named as well those in the next generation who grew up in the shadow of that war and were marked by it, and the next generation as well; if these walls included a list of the losses to history, science, art, architecture, and civilization, they would be a twin black slash across our nation; the walls would have no end.

The present fell away. There was only a thin swath of grey clouds above, rimmed in black, and my face in the polished surface. The reflection implicated me. *If this is who* we *are, then this, too, is who I am.*

The passage was a birth, telling me that a different person would emerge, as if I needed to be told.

Months later:

I sat, anonymous, in a padded folding chair behind some two hundred seated guests, in a ballroom atop Houston's Kim Son Restaurant, before floor-length red curtains and a podium on wheels. My Susan was next to me. Most of the guests were Vietnamese Americans invited there by Houston Grand Opera. Whole families had come, the children chattering in English. At the front were Sue Elliott, who had guided me through this project, and Patrick Summers, our conductor, and others now making *The Refuge* come alive.

Anthony Freud, director of the company, stepped up to the podium to give a brief welcome.

The cast assembled to sing the Vietnamese movement of *The Refuge*.

The section opens with Binh and ends with Doan, an old soldier for the South recounting his years in a prison camp. Each night, once the moon rose and the guards were asleep, the prisoners would sing the forbidden anthem of South Vietnam. I had recorded Doan singing it in his strong, quavering old voice. His eyes misted as he sang. Baritone Ryan McKinney began the anthem.

Around the room, chins came up, eyes lifted in recognition. Faces flushed, then went slack.

The tune is strictly forbidden in Vietnam today. It's a nineteenth century western-style military march, brisk and bright and shallow, a call to arms, really, evoking cavalry and snare drums, youthful faces marching forth. The song was once a symbol of a homeland sung to the brave and hopeful self, used to lead the charge to slaughter. Chris set the music at half tempo, and Ryan spooled it out in a rich and somber voice in careful Vietnamese. The effect evoked grainy images on a crackly black and white reel set at half speed, of soldiers stuck in a dreamlike slow-motion march.

Ryan's voice — it seemed he felt everything the people in that room had lived. His voice filled the room, filled us.

Around the room, backs straightened. One man rose slowly to his feet like an accordion unpleating. He squared his shoulders and raised his chin, placed a hand over his heart. As if hypnotized, another did the same, and another. Others swayed to the tune, eyes glistening with memories. Still others leaned forward in their seats and mouthed words long held in secret pockets of memory, as if they were leaning toward lost companions and lost loved ones and lost homes. Lost selves. A collective longing filled that room. Hands curled over the edges of seats, each chair an anchor in the roiling ocean.

When the old soldier had first raised his proud unsteady voice, I heard in the song his lingering identity with a vanished country. As Ryan sang it, the old anthem became a long-belated American acknowledgment of all that the people in that room had endured, a song of our badly overlapping histories and our now-shared freedom.

Or, perhaps, one soul was simply reaching out to another.

I thought, *This is home for all of us now*. How complicated their feelings about this country had to be, how compromised their sense of home. Here were people who fled because of destruction wrought by this country, *our* country — the US — their ally who failed them, and then they had run right into American arms.

What is home? A bedrock impossible notion I had held nearly all my life, a place of refuge where

I could thrive. It was a trope, really, and reality would always fall short, but the yearning that notion spawned continued in me like a waking dream. To be home, to feel at home, to have a home. Home is where you feel you are of the people around you, where you know you are an intrinsic part of a society you feel you can trust never to turn on you. *Home* is to be among people you understand because you speak their spoken and emotional and physical language; you know their song. *Home* means that you — we — own, collectively, the very dirt beneath our feet. *That's* the American Dream, that impossible elusive promise to every one of us in this country that anyone can attain their idealized home in America, land of freedom and refuge. I shared their hope that day. Then, I teetered to the other side of the hyphen in my hyphenated identity, from child of Jewish refugees to faux white American, and felt complicit in the promise of freedom we extend.

More rose to their feet. The waves rose around us. Around me, heads flung back into memories long locked away. *I was wrong*, I thought. Binh did not grow up on the other side of some fun house mirror. As I was growing up, we could not so much as glimpse the life Binh or anyone in that country lived beneath the onslaught, even if a few burning horrifying photographs that will not die gave us glimmers.

This, then, was our Venn Diagram of grief, a room full of Americans of vastly different experiences and backgrounds who sat and stood together that day within a song that, for the moment, encompassed us all, wrapped us and held us.

We may never find our way out of this music.

Old eyes grew wet. 'Of one heart we go forth, with no regret. O Citizen. O Citizen. Defend your land.'[1]

In memory of my stepfather Brian Dubin, US Air Force officer in Vietnam, who died election eve November fourth, 2008 from long-term effects of Agent Orange. He refused a military burial.

Many more told me about escaping war and its aftermath — people from Vietnam, El Salvador, Mexico, Cuba, Nigeria, Liberia, Ivory Coast, Congo, Benin, Somalia, India, Pakistan, Chechnya, the former USSR, and even one Holocaust survivor. Too often, I heard of my country raping their beloved landscape, or throwing huge sums of money and cruelly efficient arms at a corrupt government like throwing dynamite into a fire pit, and teaching men how best to kill.

---

[1] national anthem of the former South Vietnam

I came to believe that to be an American one must learn to live with this smoldering awareness ever at the uneasy edges of consciousness.

Intermezzo

Voices

From Benin Republic:
"You ask about my childhood home. I don't recommend polygamy for anybody."

From Hue, Vietnam:
"The communists used us as a shield: They came in our homes and hid on the premises; then they told the international press that the Americans bombed civilians.

"It seems now like we were always awake. I was small — if I heard any noise, I got under a chair. I was an adult before I got over that."

From Pakistan:
"After the Partition, we lived in a transit camp with no water and no sanitation. It flooded. They moved us to an army barrack, but then they needed it, and they sent us away. Then we lived in a tent camp. It burned. Then another tent camp. That's how I grew up. Now you know why I am an architect; I build hospitals."

From Vietnam:
"I felt like a plant, some weed uprooted from my birthplace and transplanted here."

From Ukraine, USSR:
"I went to work at T.J. Maxx. All day, I studied how people spoke. I would whisper customers' words to myself. I learned English very quickly."

From Vietnam:
"I bought an old sewing machine. Then, I went to the Salvation Army, and I bought shirts for twenty-five cents and jackets one dollar each. I took them home and took them apart; that's how I learned to sew. I became a very good tailor."

From El Salvador:
"Mom learned English watching Mr. Rogers. He talked so loud and clear. She cried when he died."

From Pakistan:
"I came to school, but I couldn't speak to anybody. I was shy and soft, like a tomato."

From Vietnam:
"We were immigrants, not refugees. That means we got no public assistance. We had to survive. You want to know how I feel about being an

immigrant? I'm an accountant now at Deloitte. I haven't had time to think about how I feel."

From Nigeria:
"Don't tell my story. It's too simple: Catholic family; nice home; all amenities; the good fortune to come here for an education; a job right out of school; no problem getting a green card. I spoke English; I had visited here before — my adjustment was easy. We'd get ahead and then go home.

"Then Nigeria fell apart. It was years until we could afford to go visit. When we did, I found my mother thin and ill. I thought, *Now we can take care of her*. Six months later, she died. For years, I cried. I went away and left my mom."

From Vietnam:
"When I am older and have my own home, I want my parents to come live with me, and I hope my siblings stay close. It's too easy to let a new culture take over and lose who you are."

From Chechnya, USSR:
"My father was a very social man. He worked all his life on the railroad. When we came here, we went right to work. We were so busy, and he, sick old man, no English, all the time alone in the apartment. I wished I could just show him a railroad."

From Vietnam:

"I was a boy. I always had my family around me, through sixteen months stranded on an island, and when Malay police beat us. Together, we cut wood, made shelter, found food. We stayed together in Houston, too. We lived together and worked and saved our money — it was always 'ours.'

"We leased a little restaurant. Then we opened our own. I did my homework there and had my meals. Of course, when I grew up, I gave my restaurant the names of my parents. My mother comes every day, and she bows to people as they come in the door."

Scene Three

Not From Here

I didn't know these stories would make me hear the long-muted echoes in my family, that stifled immigrant roar of loss, of children who lost their childhood, just as I didn't know that I would hear the same pinging through my country back to when the first managed to cross an ocean to our shores. To hear a whisper of *not from here* always at the back of one's consciousness now seemed to be part of being an American. Perhaps that whisper drove the tenacious American pride of ownership of the land, as if some were always saying, *We came and struggled and staked a claim — this place is ours.*

It seemed I lived among descendants of such a mixed mass of cultures and legacies, it was a wonder that we had crafted a peaceful society.
All of this led me to reach behind my family's silence and ask again, *Who are we?*

Who died a natural death, who stayed behind and got caught, who fled into Russia, who leapt from a train, who walked into the German fire and didn't return?

And who survived?

In Europe, for hundreds of years, Jews were forbidden to own land, to be part of the gentry or members of guilds that controlled nearly all industry, to engage in most professions, to marry a non-Jew unless willing to renounce their ethnicity, to hold office of any kind, to enter most universities, and far more. We were doubly and triply taxed, kidnapped for ransom, robbed and murdered without consequence, routinely locked at night in ghettos, spat on in the streets, and vilified by the church, our children often stolen and forcibly converted. We were banished from hundreds of towns and entire countries so many times that a list of banishments across centuries fills pages. In medieval times, unpaid rebel militias that historians still call 'Crusaders' marched across Europe raiding our communities for provisions as they went. They killed, raped, looted, destroyed our property, and marched on. Our women were raped by these marauders so often that rabbis ruled from then on that one's Jewishness could be verified only through the mother. The term 'Crusade' sent a shudder through Jewish history. For generations and into modern times, pogroms in Eastern Europe were the same, often ordered by the government to foment patriotism by vilifying the 'other,' a tool of hate as local police looked on.

In Western Europe, the nineteenth century brought a burst out of ghettos and into universities, and in a few countries, including Germany, a tentative move into the middle class, although antisemitism remained a norm in polite society.In Eastern Europe, Jewish ghettoizing and poverty did not change. Pogroms were a drumbeat of that life into the twentieth century. It was all a very old tradition by the time the Germans fed their war machine on Jewish wealth and silenced any complaint.

The Germans were no anomaly. We were a nation to rape for its resources. Or just to rape.

Jews lived for three hundred years in Skuodas, Lithuania alongside a Christian populace. Jews were fully half the town, but distrust was always there, a dull persistent glow. Then one day, word spread that the Germans were coming, and that's all it took. People were hungry; it was said the Germans would pay for every Jew, and the smolder burst.

They did it out of loyalty or out of fear or because old prejudices finally burned bright enough that average people allowed themselves to be swept into the mob. It was a mob of people who gave to charity and went to church and loved their children. One morning, half the town simply rose and murdered the other half — the Jewish half. They did it with kitchen knives and farm tools, swung children's heads against trees and threw babies into wells. They killed neighbors and shopkeepers they knew well who had been playmates of their childhood, a relationship across a porous divide that had been maintained for generations. With not a German in sight, one bright morning the good people of Skoadus, Lithuania murdered over four thousand men, women, and children, including the parents and aunts and uncles and cousins and neighbors and friends and lovers who my immediate family had left behind a short time before.

After three hundred years of Jews and non-Jews living together but apart in a way that allowed harassment and racist language and violence to be part of the fabric of the place, in a town where there had never been such a thing as social education or class protection by law, where both religious and lay leaders regularly used religion to justify hatred, they killed nearly all local Jews in a few hours, but then, people did the same in towns across Europe, as the Germans were coming.

Which of my family who stayed behind got to die a natural death? Who died by this mob? Who by fire, who by starvation, who by exposure in winter, who by sickness, who by bullet, who by gas?

Who of my family survived? Who fled into Russia, who leapt from a train, who hid in an attic, or a basement, or a barn, who crept into the forest like an animal, who ate leaves, who dug a hole, who crawled out of a hole, who ran between bullets and wasn't hurt? Who masqueraded? Who walked into the fire and didn't burn?

I looked for hints. I found scattered bits, a few names on graves, for those lucky enough to have been buried.

My grandfather Yaakov/Jack left Skuodas with his brother Zundel thirty years before the slaughter. The brothers were eighteen and nineteen, with just enough money in their pockets to take the first boat to anywhere. They took a train to the coast and there bought a cheap ticket to dirty, dangerous Glasgow, where a huge open-pit ironworks glowed at the center of town. Adjacent to the pit was a crowded immigrant neighborhood the locals referred to as The Gorbals, a word used today in that region to indicate abject poverty. Facades were blackened with soot, the air thick with it, every person on the street sootfaced. Children went barefoot in winter. Most of them died. Usually, it was respiratory. Jack and his brother went right to work.

The brothers had convinced the family to follow — their parents and siblings arrived soon after. One of the sisters married a Scottish man and had a child, Annie, who died at two of a respiratory infection, and so began the scatter of my family graves along a route.

Soon after Annie died, Jack left for New York to try again. He begged his Glasgow family to follow, and they did, all but Zundel, just as the woman Jack would find and marry left Skuodas for New York, and as my mother's mother, then a child, headed to New York from Poland with six sisters and their parents. The US was open to them then, which is why I am not Lithuanian or Belarussian or a Pole, and why I am not a Glaswegian. I was born in the United States because my family didn't stay behind to die.

They went to New York because they could. It was a time of sweatshops and child labor and gangs. There were no antibiotics, and no medical insurance or social welfare. There was horse dung in the streets. My family lived full lives. The children graduated college. The parents saw to that.

My mother's father, Joe, was eight when he got off the boat from Belarus with his mother and three siblings, following three years after his father left them for New York. Joe's mother was sick, made worse by the passage and the cold. She died within the year.

I don't know how Joe's father treated his orphaned children. I do know that a towering anger rooted in Joe that grew as he grew, and that he was not the only one. Joe's brother eventually robbed jewelry stores across the countryside with an automatic weapon and died in a penitentiary, and his cousin died in a gangland murder.

Which brings us to rape, a single letter step from rage, because when Joe met and married my maternal grandmother, he took his place on a family tree spattered with names I picture written in red, all men who acted out the violence and rage of their past and raped their wives and daughters across generations — a hundred fifty years of rape.

The women of previous generations that I knew in my mother's family were bonded as fellow survivors can be. Most were brilliant, astonishingly resourceful, powerfully loyal to family, and they all swore one another to secrecy. They never told Joe's real story, or their own, until their deathbeds. Their version of our family story was a rags-to-riches tale of the founding of our American family, our very own American Dream, one that erased Joe's rages, erased the existence of his criminal brother, and erased as well Joe's caustic disdain for other men and his penchant for little girls.

My family is a remnant. Immigration saved us. It concentrated the talent and determination and resilience of survivors into our remnant, but some of us have descended into mental illness, addiction… and extreme religion; there is a dark vein through the gold. A recurring need for healing is also a part of this legacy.

What losses marked us? What did we lose by leaving? A patch of land; a house; a shared language; neighbors and friends who used the same gestures and figures of speech that together formed a web of belonging; connections through which they could share with one another and ward off danger; towns (Skuodas, Lithuania; Krakow, Poland; Grodno, Belarus) in which fifty per cent and more were Jews who married one another for so many generations that I was probably related to nearly all of the Jews in each of those places, almost a hundred thousand murdered between them; gravestones in crowded cemeteries dating back centuries with our names chiseled on them in Yiddish: Mallett, Mirkus, Renner, Sidransky, Greenberg, Simon; others of our family left behind and forgotten; the names of siblings, aunts, uncles, cousins, neighbors, friends, lovers who were alive when my family departed; their stories, their stories, their stories…

As a lesbian, the Hasidim deemed my innate inclination to love irrelevant, twisted, and dangerous. I was an alien in that strict religious community living beneath an onslaught of commands to squelch my sex and sexuality, source of an ability to create, have passion, and drive, like a forced entry and attack on my being. Now I imagined I had endured a small private war, a war on my soul, then fled toward the hope of freedom.

Part Three

We Came Seeking Opportunity

Scene One

Ali (pronounced Alí), The Pakistani Patriot
Lahore, Pakistan

It was a district of identical white buildings in a monochromatic landscape of commerce and drive lacking anything inconveniently green. I sat in the car in the concrete parking lot, paused there as if listening for the heightened pulse of all of that striving. I got out and found Ali's office suite, as bare as if they had just opened for business, yet here he was in an inner office at an impressive desk. Ali was a tall man in crisp business attire, unassuming in manner, given the power he displayed from behind that desk.

Ali owned, he had told me on the telephone, fifteen gas stations, regional distributions for Shell and Texaco, a string of Burger Kings, and well, more. He had wanted to make it clear then that he was not a refugee, that he had come the United States by choice.

His assistant silently closed the door.

Ali greeted me and pointed to a chair facing him that was too large for my small frame. Behind him, the one intimation of color in the room was a globe on a stand.

"It's very hard, even for my own kids, to understand why somebody would want to leave their home, their friends and family, to make a life somewhere so different from where they grew up, but if you feel you're suffocating where you are, if you feel you can't express your feelings or your talent, if you find unmovable restrictions all around you holding you in, and you know you could do a lot more without them, you feel you must leave and never go back.

"I was a dreamer, a visionary, but in Pakistan, that's like committing a crime. Plus, I had a bad habit of questioning everything, even religion, but over there, if you say aloud in public that you reject your religion, they can kill you. It's the law.

"It got to the point that I felt like a stranger in my own country. I came to the United States on a tourist visa, but once I was here, I felt so free that I never wanted to go back. I applied for a Green Card [for permanent residency] almost immediately. That's all it took, back then — an application."

"I was born in 1961 in Lahore, a city in northeastern Pakistan on the Indian border. Lahore has enormous, beautiful buildings that were built long ago by the moguls, but they're all decaying. I visited those buildings I cannot tell you how many times. They gave me a sense of belonging to magnificence. I was amazed by their beauty and craftsmanship, and by their sheer size. They made me feel that this is my people, that this greatness is something my country was once and could still have been if the British hadn't colonized us and destroyed our institutions, but the damage was done. The British molded the Indian people into good slaves, and the founders of Pakistan kept the British system in place. The bureaucracy and military rule Pakistan as if its citizens are colonial subjects."

Pakistan is in the Indus Valley at the upper northwestern edge of the Indian continent and shares a border with India. Invaded by thirty successive empires over centuries, the area was part of India for three hundred thirty-five years under British rule. The country we know of today as Pakistan was separated from India in 1947 after India gained independence from the British. Today, Pakistan is peopled in large part by the millions of Muslims who were banished from India almost immediately after Indian independence, during the ruthless Partition; one could say Pakistan is a country born of religious violence.

From the outset, Pakistan defined itself as a specifically, defiantly Muslim state. "I think Pakistan became even worse than the British," Ali said. "The British were usurpers, but they had some sense of justice. I can't say that for my own people.

"My mother is a courageous, religious woman. She prays five times a day; she's very honest, and she never hurt anybody.

"Her father was a farmer. He married her off when she was thirteen to a man who was mentally deficient. She had three kids before she got away from him. She managed to get an education to the equivalent of eighth grade — enough to become a teacher in her village. Then she met my father. They married and moved to Lahore with the children, and there she had the six of us.

"My mother was pregnant when my father died. I was eight months old.

"My half-brother from my father's first marriage was an adult. As oldest, he inherited my father's business; my mother got nothing. He put my mother on a very low, fixed income, and she raised us, her nine children, by herself."

Ali had opened his story by speaking of his mother's courage, as if that courage was a gift she had given him to take and use to help him do what he needed in his life, which, as a man, he would be able to do. He would acknowledge this to me later. From his mother, he had learned the darker side of his privilege.

Ali was the only person in this project who opened his story with his mother, and the only man who consciously conveyed a portrait of restrictions on women in his native country.

Hemmed in by society, sold into child marriage, covered head to toe by law, forbidden birth control, denied self-agency or independent means, deprived of support by laws of inheritance, Ali's mother was left with nine children, destitute.

"There were kids from her first marriage and kids from her and my father and grown children from my father's previous marriage — twelve kids, small and grown from two different fathers and two different mothers. Growing up, I didn't have a clue who was who in the family." He laughed.

"My father ran the first law review journal in Pakistan. The high court sent all cases to his office where his lawyers would analyze them, write them up, and bind them in journals to create a record as precedent."

Similar independent review journals in the United States also publish legal cases and analyses of the rulings, and also exist to create a public record. Lawyers cite these cases as precedent to prove arguments in court; the journals have direct influence on the application of law. Ali saw his father's work as key to the function of law in Pakistan and thus a key protection of Pakistani freedom.

"The most damaging case in Pakistan's history came right after the first time the army declared military rule. The speaker in parliament filed a lawsuit to stop the military from taking over, but the Supreme Court came back with a decision that the 'Doctrine of Necessity' supersedes everything. They used this so-called Law of Necessity to give the army unlimited power and legitimize an illegitimate government. That ruling became a cornerstone for future generals. It undermined the constitution and the people's will."

The Doctrine of Necessity was a thirteenth century British maxim, yet this use of the doctrine to justify military intervention in the Pakistani government was the first instance in world history that a viable court ever used the notion to establish law. This happened in 1954, before Ali was born. Pakistan's brief exercise in democracy was over. It had lasted seven years.

"My father was remembered with respect in professional and literary circles. That set a high bar for me in society, but sometimes I hated him. I felt that being his son should have been a great thing, but instead there we were in that big house that made people think we had money. I never told anyone how poor we really were."

"One thing in my heart was always certain, and that kept me going as a boy: my mother loved me.

"Our daily routine was to go to school, come home, eat lunch, then take a nap through the hottest part of the day. In the heat, we'd draw the curtains, turn fans on, and go to sleep covered with wet sheets. After we woke up, we took a bath, put on traditional Pakistani clothes and went to learn the Koran.

"In summer, my mother arranged for a cleric to come every day and teach us to read Koran in our backyard with kids on our street. The girls sat on one side and the boys on the other. The cleric sat in the middle. He called us up one at a time and gave us a lesson.

"Our language was Urdu; the Koran is in Arabic, which we didn't understand. The cleric taught us to recognize Arabic letters and then he had us sound out the words like a robot without understanding. If you didn't pronounce a word right, he said that was a sin, and he had a cane. When I questioned him about this, he said reciting the Koran is like prayer. He said you get credit with God just by mouthing the words. He beat me many times. I hated that." Ali chuckled.

"To me, if you look at what the Muslim religion says, nobody can even come close to all that it requires of a person, so no one is truly Muslim, and yet people there are willing to die for their religion. I still don't understand that." Ali's voice had become soft with tenderness for his young self.

"When I turned fourteen, I wanted to know my purpose. I wondered, is there such a thing as destiny? Do I have a destiny? What am I meant to accomplish? I began to go to the mosque and spend time with a cleric there who was young and progressive. He gave me philosophical books by scholars that appealed to me. I got into discussions with him. I found some kind of peace."

I remembered when I first found ancient books of my people's religion, around the same age and my excitement with those heady conversations of the spirit. To get to participate in such conversations, to think aloud and be heard as a thinking person, made me feel I had arrived at adulthood. I was sure that I felt my soul seeking release, yearning for God.

"When I got older, I noticed hypocrisies in my religion and I began to ask questions. Eventually I went away from my religion even though that was very dangerous to do that in Pakistan.

"I was left with this secret guilt that I still called myself Muslim. Even as an adult, I felt maybe I never took time to properly understand my religion. I had unfinished business."

"In the family, I was just one of the kids, not the oldest or the youngest. Plus, I guess it's left from the British, but in Pakistan, the whiter you are, the more beautiful you are, and I was the only one in the family with dark skin. I had no confidence, but I had desire, and an aggressive nature. I worked hard in school. I became a leader. It helped that I grew to over six feet — that's very unique in Pakistan. To my luck, my school was co-educational. When I grew tall, girls started paying attention." He grinned.

"I wanted to go to a certain college and become a doctor, but it wasn't enough to have good grades. To get into a good school you had to know somebody. I went to my half-brother who ran my father's business. My half-brother was a resourceful and powerful man. He promised to talk to the right people.

"I asked a couple of others, but who was I? A poor widow's kid, the big dark one from the middle of the pack. Not one of the people I asked for help did what they said they would. I confronted my half-brother about it, and he shunned me.

"After our meeting, I went home and I fell on my bed, my legs hanging down, and stared at the ceiling. I realized no one was going to help me. For the first time, I saw Pakistan as a web of corruption where people only look after themselves. I decided I would never again depend on anybody else.

"I went to a different college. Then I managed to transfer over to the one I had wanted based solely on my performance. I finished my degree there and made a strong impression.

"After I graduated, I didn't know what I should do. I knew I didn't want to be a doctor. I was thinking maybe law school, but not right away.

"One day, I saw an advertisement in the paper recruiting people to become military officers. Since the military controlled our country, officers were the elite of the society. I didn't want to go into the military, but I wanted to prove my worth to my family. I took their tests, and I did very well.

"They put me in the hospital and did every kind of exam. Then they sent me to a facility in a remote area where I wrote essays and took their psychological tests and ran their obstacle courses and passed other challenges… and I got admitted. In Pakistan that is a very high achievement. Then I said, thanks, I just wanted to see if I could!

"My mother was really upset with me. She said I was throwing away my future. And my brother said, 'What is *wrong* with you?' Everyone said, 'You're crazy, why did you do that, you should take this opportunity, become one of the elite!'

I gave in."

"Very soon in my military training I understood that the military wanted to turn me into someone who would jump without thinking whenever they told me to jump. I didn't blame them — an army needs that — but I knew I didn't have it in me. They were trying to take my spirit.

"One day the major called me into his office. He spoke in English; in the Pakistani army, if you get caught speaking any language other than English you get punished. I think that's a method to make sure your slave mentality stays intact."

Ali had studied English throughout his schooling. People spoke Urdu to one another in casual conversation, but English was used in academics, for international business, and often by social climbers to impress others, as a language of power. In the army, Ali found English forced on soldiers as one might hobble a horse. In the military, English had become a language of obedience.

"The major said, 'What is wrong with you?" Then he said, 'I'll give you even more responsibility, and then you'll *have* to be more disciplined.' Right there, he promoted me to Senior Gentleman Cadet and put me in charge of a platoon.

"I stood at attention and let him talk. I didn't care what he gave me. When he was done, I walked out of his office and kept walking, away from the base and away from the army.

"It turns out, you can't just walk away from the army. That's called desertion. I realized after I did it that I had committed a crime. I had resolved not to ask anyone for favors; I went back in and admitted I had deserted. I said I was ready to take their consequences. They said my punishment was to begin my two-year term all over. I said, 'If you do that, I'll leave again,' and I walked out."

"I sat in jail with criminals and murderers. That imprisonment changed me forever. I learned that even those people have humanity in them, and that I wasn't any different from them. There are good people and there are horrible people everywhere.

"I served twenty-three days of a six-month sentence; they pardoned the rest of my sentence and sent me home stamped as damaged goods.

"Everyone at home said, 'Man, you had it made, and you blew it.' I felt so guilty that I went to law school. I lasted one semester.

"I was twenty-one when I got home from law school, and I was mixed up. I didn't know what to do with myself. I let my half-brother take me into our father's business. It turned out that was a good thing. Working there cleared my mind.

I saw a lot that I wanted to do, a lot of ways to improve efficiency. It turned out nobody there wanted to change anything, even for the good of the company. I couldn't accept that."

Ali left and started a business with a friend, making washable books for small children. The business was successful and grew quickly.

The following year, they were bought out by a large company, but the buyer delayed payout. With no liquidity, Ali and his partner couldn't produce orders on time, and this caused the business to fail. It seemed to be a strategy by the buyer to eliminate competition.

"It was impossible to get around the corruption and static systems in Pakistan. I could no longer take all the restrictions on what I thought and believed or on what I wanted to do."

Ali had discovered that business was his arena for creative thought. Freedom to utilize his talents in business was for him the same as personal freedom. Surrounded by rigidity in that arena, he felt he was choking.

"I was in a low place when I ran into my brother's friend. He was a feudal lord. I'm not kidding — there really are feudal lords in Pakistan. He invited my brother and me to come to his estate.

"The British used to find a loyal slave, give him land, then tax him heavily, but he'd get to have the entire population on his land work for him just for food and no other pay. The peasants would produce more than enough for the guy and to pay the British tax. That system is still going on.

"These landowners bar education on their lands so that they can keep their peasant tenants ignorant enough to agree to keep living as if they're enslaved. The landowners particularly make a point of preventing girls from getting an education."

Some years later, in the very area where Ali and his brother's friend met, Malala Yousefzai and two friends would be shot on their school bus by a member of the Taliban, shot because they were girls daring to attend school.

"Then the landowner boasted to me that he knew someone in the American Consulate. I immediately said, 'Really? Can you get me a visa?' I knew I wanted to go. And he said, 'Sure.'"

"The first thing I did when I got to Kennedy Airport was, I sat down in a diner and ate a hamburger that was not halal, it wasn't blessed, and I didn't care how it had been slaughtered. That hamburger was my first act of freedom."

I laughed out loud. One of the first things I did after leaving the Hasidim was declare shrimp kosher.

Islam and Judaism both have strict rules about what the faithful eat. Similar to the kosher laws, Islam requires that animals are to be ritually slaughtered in a special process that kills them instantly with minimal pain. In both traditions, these laws are meant to make the simple act of eating an intrinsic part of the life of the spirit, to raise us above our physical hunger, in part by holding us responsible for the animal's pain and thus heightening our sensitivity to suffering, with every bite. It's a beautiful notion. Unfortunately, rigid rules can become a purpose unto themselves, obeyed by numbed soldiers of God for the sake of obedience alone, until the original humanity and hopeful spirit behind the rules fades away. That potential failing, I believe, is a key spiritual challenge to the devoted.

"Somehow, until I got to the United States, I didn't realize how dangerous it was for me in Pakistan. I only understood the danger when I left and saw how freely people here do things and talk and make decisions. I saw, and right away I knew I wanted to stay.

"My brother was living in Dallas. I flew there from New York to join him. He gave me a pillow and blanket, and I slept on the floor.

"Next morning, my brother shook me awake and said, 'You can stay three weeks for free. Get your driver's license, get a social security number, and find a job, because after that, you're going to pay me rent, groceries, and utilities.' I hated him for that, but that was the best thing he could have done."

I asked Ali, "May I ask what was in your suitcase?" I was thinking how objects brought across the ocean often become precious.

A slow smile spread across Ali's face. "Besides dirty clothes? Gifts sent by my mom: cassettes of Pakistani music, our traditional clothing, and our typical sweets. I also brought drawings I made when I was a teenager."

He looked thoughtful.

"You know, music, food, and clothing are the things that change the most for us."

Music, food, and clothing — that's culture, sustenance, and identity, sent by his mother, as if she was saying, *Don't forget who you are.* In his young drawings Ali would always recognize the teen with a questing mind.

"I had ten dollars in my pocket and my big dreams," he said. Then looked down at the desk.

"I also brought bitter memories. I felt my country had abandoned me. I'm still heartbroken about that. Pakistani people are good people, but their whole life is about working to succeed and feel they belong under an inescapable law. The system pulls them into this whirlpool where survival is the only game.

"When I think of the negative reactions of my friends and family when I left, I tell myself, in such an environment, when you're trying to survive it can be a luxury to be kind."

He sighed. "People are just people."

"I absolutely, blindly fell in love with this country. I wanted to become one hundred per cent American, even more so than the Americans.

"The first thing I remember noticing is how, if you meet someone's eyes on the street, they smile and say hello. That blew me away. People feel free here and not afraid.

"My first job was in a Burger King. They paid me $4.85 an hour, and it was great. Then, I took a second job on the graveyard shift at a Seven Eleven for $6.00 an hour. I worked both until Seven Eleven offered me a lot of overtime at time and a half. I would work eighteen hours straight, go home, sleep, eat, and go back. It was exciting to collect that paycheck. I even saved up enough to buy an old car.

"After a while, I decided to move out. My brother didn't like that. I had been paying him every month, helping with the bills, but I figured he'd be okay, and you know, he was.

"I got my own place, and I added a paper route. Every night after work, I drove a hundred miles delivering papers. I was paying rent and saving to go to college.

"I also joined a cricket team."

Ali joined one of the many lively all-male immigrant soccer and cricket leagues in the area. They were strong social groups and a great source of networking. I thought of them as the poor man's golf.

"One day, we played a team from Houston, and I ran into a childhood friend! We talked for a while. I told him I was starting to get tired of working so much. He said there were better jobs in Houston.

"I went and told my brother, and my brother said, 'Let's move there.' It was like we'd been tossed out together and had to stay together. If I was going, he was going to go, too, and that's what we did."

In Houston, Ali's brother got into law school. Ali continued to work at minimum wage. His financial situation wasn't much better than in Dallas.

"One day, a guy I met playing cricket said, 'Hey, I'm buying a gas station, and I want you to manage it.'

Ali had obviously made an impression.

"He said the station was failing. I said, 'I don't know anything about gas stations.'

"You know, I figured it out. For the next year, I operated that place like it was mine, and I turned it around. The Mobil rep was impressed. One day, she showed up and told me they had a station they wanted to sell. She asked if I was interested. She said the deal required a hundred thousand dollar investment.

"I had no money. I said 'Yes.' Then I went straight to my friend who gave me the job and told him, 'Invest what I need and after I earn back your investment and pay you back, we'll be partners fifty-fifty.'

"I bought him out in 2003. I paid him over two million dollars.

"I thought I'd achieved the American Dream. I never wanted to go back to Pakistan. I felt, just give me the freedom and the opportunity and I'll make things happen."

"When I first got to Houston, while I was still working odd jobs, I met this girl, and we dated three years. She was the best thing that had ever happened to me. We were soulmates. I was working a lot of hours, but we were happy. We didn't have to go out and spend money — we'd get a bottle of wine, cook dinner together, and listen to music. It amazed me that she was from a totally different background from me, and still we connected so well, although sometimes she'd laugh at my Pakistani music.

"She wanted to get married. I didn't know if I was ready, but I knew I loved her.

"I hadn't been able to bring myself to tell my family about her. Then my mother came to visit, and she stayed with my brother. While my mother was in town, I said, 'Yes, I'll marry you;' then I went over and told my brother and mother.

"My mother refused to meet her or to stay for a wedding. Later that day, my oldest brother called from Pakistan and said, 'If you marry her, I'll never speak to you again.'

"We got married in Vegas." He laughed.

"I was never totally honest with my wife about my family's rejecting her. I just told her, 'You know, they'll be fine,' and in time, they were. Eventually my brother and mother came from Pakistan to meet her.

"Living together turned out to be not such a good thing. When Pakistani friends came over and we sat around speaking in Urdu, she'd say, 'You all know English. Why would you speak another language in my home?'

"I tried to explain to her that it feels good when you find people who speak your own language, that you can't translate jokes and cultural stuff and so many little things. I told her when you can speak your language you feel at home, but she said she felt like we intended to exclude her in her own place."

Ali didn't seem to understand what this did to his wife. Right there in the house that he and his wife jointly owned, he would revert to his own culture and language and exclude her, as if he was saying, 'My language is my truer home.'

Listening to this, I thought, *If only their home could have been a new kind of amalgam where each could be totally themselves, yet the whole became something else altogether, with a new language that reflected them both. Something like America.*

However, a new language would not have comforted Ali with memories of home.

The two also had different conceptions of marriage.

"There are things in my culture that were small for me, but they were a big deal for her. Like, a

Pakistani wife would never have a problem with her husband working all the time, and would never think to call him at work, but she called me at work every day. I'd just say, 'I'm tied up,' and not think anything of it."

She was lonely and frustrated. Once day, Ali came home, and his wife asked him to move out. Ali was shocked.

"That killed me. She was my wife!"

To him, the very word 'wife' meant duty, loyalty.

"I left our home with nothing but a suitcase of clothes, just like when I left Pakistan. I got in my car and went to ten different places until I found an apartment. The first night, I slept on bare carpet without so much as a blanket or pillow; I didn't even have what my brother gave me that first night. I lay there and cried.

"You know, I learned something. In any culture, there are things that are understood but not spoken. Back home in Pakistan, you knew your place in life. There's a place for a mother, a brother, a friend — an understood status and role for every man and woman. She didn't understand any of that.

"I decided I'm never getting married again."

I stifled a laugh.

"When I turned thirty-three, I decided to go back and visit Pakistan. I had decided that, for my marriage to last, it had to be with someone from home; I knew my mother and sister would be waiting with a girl for me."

Ali went home willing to take part in ritual matchmaking, but he went as a quasi-outsider. He participated with wry humor and just a touch of good-natured rebellion, from the formal first meeting of the families, the brief and chaperoned first sighting of his bride, through the elaborate wedding and post-wedding escort back to Houston. He did it all with love, embracing the identity he had fled. He told me he now felt both American and Pakistani.

The pendulum had swung — right, left, middle ground. Ali was more carefully balanced now on the hyphen of his newly hyphenated identity. He understood how his roots had formed him and remained part of him. He saw Pakistan as his past and America as his future, his new mindset, his hope.

"I got very lucky. My wife is a wonderful person."

"It was hard for my wife when I brought her here. She didn't know this country, she didn't speak English, and I was traveling a lot. She resented me pushing her to do American things. Also, she was afraid to drive."

I looked up, raised my eyebrows. "You wanted a Pakistani wife, and you wanted her to become American," I said.

"Just not too American," he said.

We both laughed. "That old hyphen," I said. "Ever feel like you're teetering on it, right there in the middle?"

"For a while, I thought I might have made the biggest mistake of my life. It took my wife three years to understand that I wasn't being mean. Then she started playing tennis and made friends on the court. She learned how to drive. We had a daughter, and another. The girls grew, and she started to volunteer in their school. Now she speaks English, and she has friends. She wears short skirts and everything. I think she's happy. She seems happy. I know I am."

Somehow, this took me back to Ali's mother. His mother had made him conscious of the freedom he wanted for his wife. He would do for his wife what he could not do for his mother's life — he would set her free.

"One guilt remained: I was an adult, but I didn't have an adult understanding of my religion. I was born a Muslim. That was supposed to be part of me.

"In the month of Ramadan, Muslims don't eat from dawn to dusk. All that month you are supposed to be careful not to sin or lie. You are supposed to start every day with a ritual bath, then say prayers. You pray and recite the Koran five times a day.

"I decided to try that, but this time, when I recited the Koran, I would make sure I understood every word.

"First day, I got up before sunrise. I showered, I ate in the dark, I said prayers at dawn as I was supposed to do; then I took an English-language Koran in my hands. I held it up, and I said, 'God, I am about to read your holy book. Give me the wisdom and light it contains so that I can live a good life.'

I opened the book and started reading out loud. They say the Koran is study and prayer in the same breath, so it is supposed to be holy to read it out loud.

"Reading it out loud made me think about it more carefully. The more I read, the more questions I had, and the more questions I had, the more I remembered that as a child I was told if you asked a question, that's the work of the devil.

"I'm not a child, and I live in America now. I have learned to think freely. That's the best gift this country has given me, the best gift anybody could give anyone: to feel like a free man with my own mind, to be able to think like a free man. When you have that, you will never let anybody take it away from you.

"All day each day, I let myself think into the questions that came up for me as I read the Koran. By the end of two weeks of fasting and praying and then reading and thinking like this, I had found so many contradictions, and so much of what I read conflicted with my personal values, that I decided, not only is the Koran not written by my God, it isn't written by any God I knew of. I put it away.

"Since then, I've read the Bible enough times to know I can't believe that one, either. I've done a lot of soul-searching and come to the conclusion that there may be a God, but I don't think there's a religion that God sent to man. If God sends a religion that demands we pray to him and honor him, that's self-serving. You can't make the rules yourself, then appoint yourself judge. That's like a judge being party to his own case."

This sent me instantly to the young man in Pakistan learning the function of law in his father's business.

"Religions are theories. I believe in the possibility of God, but no one can prove God.

Besides, if I chose to believe in any one thing, I would be dismissing all other possibilities, but I won't dismiss something that is still possible. I won't accept any absolute."

He sighed. "I am Pakistani. I tried to change that in America, but that's who I am. I rejected my religion. I reject all predetermined beliefs. I can and I will be my own judge."

Ali decided to study the United States Constitution and the structure of American government. Soon, he was teaching civics after hours at his daughters' high school and leading discussions about the role of government. The conversations with students gave him great satisfaction. He was getting to clarify American freedom to people who were just beginning to understand what it was to live as an adult in the world. He felt they should know their rights and use them from the beginning of stepping out into the world. He wanted them to appreciate their amazing democracy.

"Then came 9/11. All that day, I thought I was going to throw up, not only because of the attack, but also because the people who did that were believed to have a connection to me. My world turned upside down. I was horrified at this guilt by association. I couldn't imagine what to expect next.

The attack brought people together, but I felt absolutely alone.

"My American-born friends called all that day to ask if I was okay. Their calls were nice, and I appreciated them, but they didn't help."

"Just before we went to war in Iraq, one of my vendors invited me to go with him on a hunting trip. I said, 'I don't kill animals.' He said, 'It's just a good time outdoors,' and I went.

"Our first night out, we grilled steaks and had a few drinks. Then we started talking politics. I said, 'I think the president is rushing into this war. I think the people in our government have their own agenda.' I said, 'We're mistaken to compare Iraq with Germany and Japan after the Second World War. Iraq is far from homogeneous like those countries were; there are many factions this dictator has kept under control. I think those factions will make a lot of trouble now.'

"Monday morning in my office, the telephone rings at my desk, and a man on the other end says, 'Sir?' I say, 'Yes?' He says, 'This is the FBI.'"

My heart stopped.

"He said, 'I understand you went on a hunting trip.'

"I thought, man, I didn't have a permit. That's what scared me. I swallowed, and I said, 'Yes, I did.'

"He said, 'You called our president a warmonger.'

"Then, I got some courage. I said, 'I don't believe the president is doing the right thing pushing us into war, and last time I checked, it was still constitutional in this country to say what you believe.'

"The agent said, 'Yes, sir, but under the circumstances…'

"I said, 'Listen. The only reason you called me is because of where I'm from and the religion you think I have. But just because I was born in Pakistan doesn't mean I love this country any less. I know a lot more about American history, its culture, and the Constitution than a lot of people, and unlike people who were born here, I *chose* this country. I want my kids to have the freedom I fell in love with. Once you have that, you don't ever give it up.'

"I said what he was doing was McCarthyism, witch-hunting. I told that guy, 'Where I come from, I didn't have the freedom to say what I believe and I'm not letting you take that away from me here.'

"The man said, 'Sir, we are required to follow up on every lead. I won't bother you again.'

"It didn't end there. That agent didn't call again, but he left my name on a list, and others called. I told the first few the same thing. Then, they started asking about my employees. I gave one of them a copy of my payroll; I felt I had to, and well, maybe that made them decide I really am loyal because the next one asked me to snitch on people as if I was their route into the Pakistani community. I told him, 'I don't know anyone involved in anything wrong, and if I did, I'd report it to the police, not you. I'm not working for you.'

"The last time an FBI guy came, he brought me a book about Lahore signed by the author, full of pictures of those beautiful old buildings. I pushed it back across the desk, and I said, 'I'm not helping you.'"

Ali's whole demeanor had changed. His shoulders hung a little lower, his face a picture of concern. He looked resigned.

"Until 9/11, I felt this was my home, but I've changed. Now, when I go visit Lahore, I feel like an alien there, while here in this country, there is a stereotype attached to me. I'm not completely at home here, either.

"This is still my home, but I have new doubt that bothers me. It's doubt I'd rather not have, but I think I can't get rid of."

In the same innocent way that Ali had loved his first wife, he had loved America. That was what I heard in his voice that day — the sound of a jilted lover.

Today, I would not expect an FBI agent to politely question Ali over the telephone. Neither would Ali get to use his knowledge, his patriotism, his eloquence, and his considerable integrity to convince an FBI agent of his rights. Instead, faceless ICE agents could pick him up, take him to some undisclosed place where no one could reach him or even find him, charge him on a technicality that just might be fictional, and quite possibly deport him. Our world has already changed.

Today I wish I could take Ali's love of our country to Americans young and old of every color and gender, to people whose families have forgotten their roots and to those who have just arrived. I would ask every one of them to please, please read how Ali fell in love with America because *everyone here feels so free, not afraid of anything.* I would say, all of these years after Ali told his story, please tell me what he found here is still true.

I left my home in the religious community. I left my two youngest, boys in their teens. I left nearly all of my friends. I left my adopted culture and its language, so that some of my adult children felt I had left them as well. I left my community, our shared history, and intertwined lives. I left our gestures and figures of speech, our rituals and sacred texts that guided and soothed us. I left our mode of dress, the lowered gazes of women. I left the prayers that crept often to our lips. I left our God.

I stepped out alone, the first time I had ever been alone, and I ran toward American freedom. I ran to a country where a lesbian wasn't allowed to marry and couldn't move freely without threat, but for little white me, the dream of a fair-enough system held.

No more passive shock. After Ali, every step I took through areas of the city new to me, every time I let someone take me away with their stories, every time I felt connected through this project to someone I would otherwise never have gotten to know, was an act of seizing my new world and making it mine. With each new person, I thought, *This is us*. I thought, *Compared to so many, how small my upheavals, my so-called efforts*.

I would become a devoted traveler.

Intermezzo

Voices

From the Democratic Republic of Congo:
"In my country a cab driver was a poor man. Here in the US, a cab driver is a rich man — he can feed his family *and* pay his bills!"

From Nigeria:
"I came to Sharpstown High, and kids said, 'Are you from Africa? You a monkey? And what's a refugee, anyway?'"

From Mexico:
"I got married to a man from El Salvador. We loved each other, but it was like he was a temporary worker. He slept on the couch; he let friends use his car; he fed them, and they fed him, and he sent most of his money to his family in El Salvador. That wasn't a home."

From Mexico City:
"I felt like I left this huge cosmopolitan city and came to a backwater. In front of my high school

class, my history teacher asked me, 'Have people in Mexico ever heard of Elvis?' I thought, *Do you people think I lived under a rock?*

"In history, the topic was immigration. The kids thought immigrants were all uneducated laborers. I knew so many who came here who had a good education, but they were working blue-collar jobs because they didn't have the right papers or enough English. I'd been sheltered in a lot of ways, but it seemed my classmates knew jack about the world if it didn't have to do with Texas."

From Nigeria:
"America opened my mind, made me see it is possible to have a society where you get paid for what you do, and with that, you can pay rent, and eat, and feel safe in your bed. Not like Africa, where a man works every day, and with one month's pay, he buys water, and that is all."

From the USSR:
"In Russia, my children could never have accomplished what they have accomplished here. This is a beautiful country, in spite of all the lawyers who are here."

From Pakistan:
"You can't say living in the States allowed me to be a doctor because I did my medical training in

Pakistan. Or that a woman is freer to practice medicine here. That's just not true. But something changed in me after I came here. I married, divorced, buried my mother. Pakistani friends say, 'Look at her, miserable woman, no children, alone, a terrible life without a man,' but I love my life. Is it that independence that you call American?"

Same person from Mexico City:
"The World Cup was playing in Mexico when we got to Houston, but nobody here gave a damn about soccer. That was the first shock."

From Democratic Republic of Congo:
"I miss the connections. That's the best way to put it — the automatic connections I felt with people back home, and the freedom I felt with them. Here in the States, I have to keep my guard up all the time. No matter how long I live here, I'm a kind of guest, never free to misbehave, because if I did, they would call me a Black man, and an immigrant."

From Mexico:
"I took my children to the park. They are not so dark like me, and someone said, 'How much do you charge to babysit? I want to know, can you be my maid?'"

From El Salvador:

"I love the values in this country. I'm happy that I got married here to a man who respects me as a human being. I don't have to be submissive, or passive. As I get older, my experience will be valued, and I won't be fired for someone younger to do the job. There are safeguards here.

"Look, it's not perfect, but I came without English. We lived on WIC [food supplements for impoverished women and infant children], free milk and bread, public schools. I slept at a neighbor's place while my mother worked three jobs, and still I got my education and a career — me, little refugee kid, settled and safe. The sky's the limit. You really can aim to be anything you want to be."

Scene Two

Mythili and Murthy, *Karnataka, India*

After my years of communal life, I was living alone among strangers in an enormous apartment complex, a march of identical red doors that stretched for blocks, behind each the same butcherblock kitchenette, white stippled walls, and worn beige-and-brown carpeting. My unit was furnished with secondhand furniture.New friends said the place looked like I was camping out. I may have been trying to navigate a society that had moved on without me, may have needed to learn how to buy insurance, master a remote control, and make sense of the images marching across my screen, but whenever I felt out of sync, I reminded myself that I had a place of my own, a car in my own name, work that I loved, and a variety of choices now mine alone.

As to the neighbors, we were cordial yet careful in a kind of anonymous intimacy. I counted on the constants in this place: the smell of curry outside one of the doors on any given day, and the man who padded mornings to the mailboxes in sagging pajama bottoms and a sleeveless undershirt over his bulging middle who always dropped a gruff hello.

One evening, I parked in my numbered slot and made my way to the front of the complex as the sound of a violin wafted down from somewhere on an upper floor; scales, arpeggios, etudes, all played with a doggedness that made me think of parents with high expectations. I pictured the violinist also studying for SATs under the parents' watchful eyes. Another day, I heard the music and thought of my grandmother's violin from her young years, the one my grandfather Joe found and sold. This time, I followed the sound. I found the door. I knocked.

A barefoot girl-woman answered, instrument in hand. She was seventeen or so, with long, wavy dark hair and bright intelligent eyes. I caught a glimpse of a mat just inside, on it, a pair of well-used sandals. "I live downstairs," I said, trying to claim that stranger/neighbor status I thought might legitimize the knock.

"Hi," she said.

An unspoken question hovered between us.

"I heard you play."

There was an awkward moment. I tried to explain, using buzz words like 'opera' and 'immigrants,' thinking them effective. Before she could close the door, I quickly added that if her family would talk with me, they wouldn't have to disclose their names. She said, "I'll... tell my parents?"

Next day, I found a note on my door in an elegant hand. A few days later, I met the parents, Mythili and Murthy. I left my sandals on the mat.

Mythili handed me a steaming mug of black tea, then settled across from me in a padded chair next to her husband. She seemed relaxed, possibly bemused, her eyes as lively as her daughter's. In contrast, Murthy looked a bit stiff. He gave a polite nod to acknowledge my presence, his expression serious. I thought the two a bit oddly matched.

Like many who had come from India, Mythili and Murthy had arrived in the United States without a last name and found they were required to declare one. Others from India in that situation used the name of their town or sub-caste as a last name — Patel, for example, a sub-caste of farmer landowners. Murthy's solution had been to split up his given name. Gopalakrishnamurthy thus became Gopalakrishna Murthy, at least legally, and Mythili became Mythili Murthy. This made them laugh in the telling, given the happy relief that they had managed to cross into this country and hold onto their names. That was a comfort in a new place, even if Murthy was left having to ask people to address him by his last name.

Murthy had entered the US on a J-1 Special Exchange Visa for scientists. Mythili came as a spouse without a work permit. Both had multiple college degrees, Mythili's in library science, Murthy's in material science and solid-state chemistry. Murthy worked in a research lab at the University of Houston.

Maybe it was the violin, or the tea, lonely me, or the fact that I sensed something incongruous about the pair. I already knew that I wanted their story.

Murthy wasn't at all sure. "What is it you are looking for?" he said.

"Not one thing in particular," I said. Then, I was left trying to explain to this research scientist that I began every interview without a focus or a goal. "I listen for the unexpected," I said.

Murthy looked quizzical.

A week later, my shoes were again on the mat, another steaming cup in my hand. The violinist daughter came out for a brief hello, and I met Meenakshi more properly before she slipped back to her homework.

"Can you help me with context?" I asked Murthy. I had met people from different cultures from all over the Indian continent. "There is so much to India."

"Well, we're Brahmins," Murthy said.

"Should I assume you are vegetarians?"

In the system of social castes that still marks India, Brahmins are descendants of ancient scholars and leaders, and as far I understood, often members of the upper class. Many (not all) are vegetarians.

"Oh yes, that we are. Vegetarians," Murthy said. He and Mythili both nodded. "From the sub-caste Madhva." He gestured to an image on the wall near the kitchen that looked like a framed print of a very old painting. In it, an Indian holy man posed in the manner of a Buddha solemnly holding up two fingers. Madhvacharya's thirteenth-century philosophy delves into the ways in which one can attain wisdom — within yourself, from observing the world, or by learning from the wise. Apparently, Murthy had made the pursuit of knowledge his life.

"Pictures of Madhvacharya always show him with two fingers raised," Murthy said. "He's pointing to the duality of man and God. Man and God are not the same," he intoned, "but one can attain godhood."

I felt Murthy was attempting to show me his ideal self; what, or who, he wished to be.

Mythili nodded her head at a slight angle in a dip of acknowledgement. "Growing up in a Brahmin household wasn't so different from anyone else's childhood," she said, as if trying to normalize the story for me. "There were a few things besides no meat or alcohol. The biggest was absolute respect for parents and teachers. You did not question them." She dipped her head again to soften the statement. "My family wasn't particularly strict, and they were never unkind," she said. She smiled with fondness, remembering. "Hinduism guides; it does not obligate or punish."

I took a sip of my tea. It's not that I doubted Mythili's portrait of her gentle parents and their gentle religion. It's just that I had seen religion take on the character of those who wielded it. I thought of a Muslim man from India I had met for this project who was sent as a child by train to Pakistan during the Partition. He gave me a child's eye view through automatic doors of a train car that opened at every stop to murderous Hindu mobs wielding machetes and piles of Muslim dead heaped on the platform, just before the doors closed again.

"How did you two meet?" I said. "Was it a love marriage?" I knew the term as once vaguely scandalous in India, used for a marriage that came about only because of mutual desire without traditional Indian matchmaking; love American style.

"No!" Mythili laughed. "You know, I used to tell my parents, 'Not me! I'm going to have a love marriage,' but we're Hindus. You accept what life brings." This time the dip of her head seemed more a gesture of resignation.

"It's not that I had to reconcile myself to marrying someone I didn't know," she said. "It's more like I had no concept that I might have any control. All my life, I was taught to trust that my parents would find someone for me. Then one day, I came home from work and my mother said they'd found a boy. No, they never asked me what kind of boy I wanted. They told me what *they* wanted: someone highly educated from a good family. You never said no to your parents, whether you agreed or not."

I wondered if she did agree.

"That's what my parents looked for as well," Murthy said. He sounded self-satisfied, and sweetly pleased with his wife. I imagined an awkward boy, his head full of science. "My parents wanted a girl from a good family. Good social standing. Good character," he said. "I was a graduate student. Like a lot of young men from nice families, I'd never been on a date. I'd never been alone with a girl."

"My parents invited his family to our house," Mythili said. "They sent the two of us upstairs, but then we were alone together."

Murthy actually blushed. "It felt strange, sitting with a strange girl. It felt strange speaking with a strange girl."

"Here to marry me!" Mythili said, a little shock in her voice. "Right away, he said he wanted to go abroad. Oh, that scared me!" She looked at Murthy as if from a distance. "After he left with his family, I told my parents I was not keen on him. I told them I had a different idea of what my husband should be like, but they just said, 'He'll be good for you.'"

Murthy looked a little dreamy-eyed. "I wouldn't allow myself to get excited since it wasn't my decision," he said. "I knew I had to be prepared for a no, but I had a feeling she'd say yes."

"Thousands came to the wedding. Her family was in debt for years. I didn't want that for them," Murthy said.

"I admired Murthy for trying to keep the wedding simple, but my father wouldn't listen," Mythili said.

Then came the drone of the music, the tumult of celebrants in the streets, and amidst that, one bedecked and bangled bride in sari red with her equally bedecked groom carried high straight to their unchosen destiny.

"The wedding lasted for days," Mythili said. "Afterwards... I'd never lived apart from my parents before. The day that I left home, I wouldn't let go of my grandmother. I was very attached to her.

"We were expected to live in his parents' house the first six months. That was awkward. I ran often to my parents."

It was nice to hear how Mythili held to her attachments while still conforming to all those expectations, but I was thinking of how foreign this scripted life in an American context. How fiercely we wield our precious freedom of choice in this country that has no overarching ancient culture, no modifying script. Then I was a young person in a world of too many choices and no guidance, lacking the wisdom to choose well on my own. I reached for a tradition-bound life then as an anchor. I thought, *Maybe it wasn't such a bad choice, at the time.*

"I'd been living on campus in a dormitory," Murthy said. "I'd eat at the mess and go home when I wanted. Now I had to go home every day to my wife, who I didn't know, and in my parents' home!

"Then it came, the offer I had hoped for: a position in postdoctoral research at a university in Illinois. Of course, I accepted."

I noticed he said *I* rather than *we*.

"While we waited for our visas, we packed our things and spent time with our families," Mythili said. "It was unusual to go away from your family, even temporarily. We planned to stay in the States three years."

"Then we came. What a shock!" Murthy said.

"I came here with a stranger," Mythili said.

"She didn't know how to cook!"

"He didn't know how to drive!"

"We got here in January. Neither of us had ever seen snow."

"We had no coats! An Indian colleague of Murthy's called and told us, 'Go right now and buy milk, tomatoes, onions, and coats from Sears.'"

I laughed.

"We'd never seen a supermarket," Murthy said.

"We were used to milk from cows, not cartons," Mythili said. "Only the vegetables looked familiar, and we didn't know how to pay!

"Back home, my grandmother did all the cooking. She never taught me how. When I'd ask, she'd say, 'Go read a book.' There's this soup with lentils and tomatoes that we like; I tried to make it; then I kept saying, 'This isn't how it's supposed to taste.'" She shrugged. "He never complains."

"I got used to pizza," Murthy said drily.

"He never complains," Mythili said.

"I got used to it."

Pizza.

Alone together for the first time, Mythili and Murthy were newly dependent on one another as sole support, and for the warmth they had previously gotten from their families.

"We'd jumped into so much," Mythili said.

"I worked all the time," Murthy said.

"I wasn't allowed to work," Mythili said, "and he was never home."

Mythili had come as a spouse on a temporary visa and did not have a work permit. Her voice dropped, remembering that period of new immigrant loneliness.

"At first, I felt terrible," she said. "Then I enrolled in the university. I took classes in computer science and French. I loved being back in school. I also joined the Indian student organization, and my English got better. I even became an announcer on their radio program!" She grew quiet. "We had left our family," she said. Her tone made doing so sound outrageous.

Murthy said, "My mother has fourteen grandchildren, and I don't know how many great-grandchildren. Nearly all of them live near her, and they come to her house all the time. If we'd stayed in India, as the oldest in my family, I would have had to take over my father's business and support all of my siblings. That's what you do there. I would never have accomplished the things I've accomplished here."

Ultimately, it was Murthy who preferred a world that wasn't tradition-bound, where he felt most free to pursue his goals and expand his mind. The two decided to stay in the United States.

I always wanted to know, where do newcomers go when they flounder? What structure can they rely on? The two looked shyly at one other.

"We had no one else to turn to," Mythili said. "We turned to each other."

"We became partners here," Murthy said.

"We needed each other so much! You could say that our life together began here."

"Our home is our little world."

Then Mythili found she was pregnant. They were overjoyed.

"I put out many applications," Murthy said. "The University of Houston offered me a good position. We wouldn't miss the snow."

"The climate in Houston would be more like India," Mythili said. "We packed all our things in the car and drove there. It was a chance to see our new country." She smiled. "Murthy drove very, very carefully." They crossed the mid-continent prairie and the river-timbered Arkansas mountains, through the dense old pine forests of northeast

Texas dotted with little towns, some of them dying, then south through the Texas Hill Country, over broad, flat farmland dotted with mesquite and dogwood, and down to the sprawling coastal city.

"Houston was big — too big," Mythili said, "but the Indian scene here was like finding a little town of friends in the middle of the big city. A friend of a friend — someone we didn't even know — gave us a place to sleep until we found this apartment."

They moved in and stayed. Meenakshi was born, and grew.

"This is a city of immigrants," Murthy said. "Everywhere I look, I see someone from somewhere else. That, I think, is what makes this country great."

I thought of the US in that moment as a blank canvas for an array of people newly cut free from so many worlds of expectations. I thought of the eager exuberance in that, and the desperate kind of ingenuity that can come with it. Then Murthy sat up a little straighter.

"We are Hindus," he said, lest I think he had forsaken his ties. "We remain vegetarians, we put aside food for the poor from every meal, and we do not drink or smoke." He pulled his collar aside then to reveal a sacred, specially-knotted cotton string that was considered a mark of nobility reserved for the Brahman caste. "I always wear it," Murthy said.

He described his Hindi *upanayana* ceremony back in India when the sacred string was bestowed upon him. He was nineteen. "The ceremony swore me to scholarship, charity, piety, and loyalty to my people," Murthy said. "I wear it always to remember who I am." It seemed to be telling me, *I didn't betray myself or my people by coming here, I'm just... a little different now.*

At this point in this work, I found Murthy's need in his adopted country to hold onto a symbol of his roots so common, I saw the string as a mark of an American.

My Hasidic boys and their father each wore, beneath their shirts, a large square of cloth with a hole in it for the head and hanging, knotted strings tied to each corner. This is the ritual *tzitzith* fringes that fly at the waist in clichéd pictures of dancing Hasidim. The garment was meant to be worn as a private, constant reminder of faith and a reminder of their Jewish identity, much like Murthy's Hindi version. Suddenly, to my *who am I now* came Murthy's silent response: "I am an amalgam, someone *I* get to define. At my core (he fingers the knotted thread) I know where I'm from."

"And Meenakshi?" I said.

Mythili said her daughter attended the public high school that was nearby. "Meenakshi has friends from all over the world," she said.

"Do you allow her to date whoever she wants?"

Murthy frowned. "I want our daughter to marry an Indian boy. I want to feel comfortable with him and to understand him."

"I won't allow an arranged marriage for our daughter," Mythili countered. "I was brought up never to say no to my parents, whether I agreed or not, but that's not Meenakshi."

I smiled. Mythili and Murthy were both assuming they had some level of control about the choices their American daughter would make about love.

It seemed Meenakshi was already caught up in her generation's dance with tradition. I felt certain that, like Ali, she would find she had options on either side of that proverbial hyphen.

Mythili grew quiet. Was she transported just then to that day in bridal red when she was carried into her future under the expectant gazes of an entire town? It seemed she could see now how the girl she once was had lost her choices about love long before her birth. Yet Mythili had been misty-eyed remembering her arranged marriage. She had stayed the path. "What changed for you?" I asked.

"Do you mean, what made me change?" she said.

"Maybe," I said. "I guess, when you move across the world and adopt a new place, you can't help but change." I thought, *Whatever your answer, this will shape your daughter.*

Mythili grew quiet. "What changed me? Oh, just... time," she said. She looked off somewhere far away. Maybe she was thinking about her years of trying to adjust and inadvertently changing herself in the process. Maybe there was no one thing or condition that had changed her. Maybe everything had changed.

"Some days," Mythili said, "I feel like I don't belong anywhere, and some days, I feel like I belong to the whole world. Am I Indian or am I American?"

She wasn't questioning either her Indian or American citizenship, or pondering where to put her loyalty, or trying to arrive at just one identity. She seemed to speak her question as a statement, a question that remained and was to remain a question.

I thought, *This could be something Mythili has asked herself many times,* the 'Who am I now?' that so many immigrants ask themselves. *Maybe she will pass that very question on to her daughter and possibly to a grandchild, as my family had.*

"I've lived half my life in this country," Mythili said. "Of course, I've changed, but sometimes I feel like, because I'm here, I'm somehow more Indian than before."

Their arranged marriage had turned into a love marriage. Far from home, Mythili and Murthy had found that holding one another was a way to hold onto their lost world. Theirs was an American love story, immigrant style.

As I handed Mythili my empty mug and slid my feet back into my sandals, I was rocketed back to my first awkward meeting with the man I was supposed to marry, and to our elaborate Hasidic wedding when two shocked strangers were transported straight into that prescribed life. Since leaving the Hasidim, I had thought of arranged marriages as a thievery of choice, thought of strict religion as autocracy in which women always pay, but as I walked away from Mythili and Murthy's place that day, I thought of how, for those two, memories of their arranged marriage formed a sweet connection to tradition that they treasured. Perhaps, when it comes to tradition and religion, it's not always either/or. Besides, in end, they did get to choose. They chose one another.

The difference between my arranged marriage and theirs? Like Ali and his Pakistani bride, Mythili and Murthy found in America the freedom to soften prescribed roles and make choices together as equals.

Walking back to my apartment, Mythili's '*Am I Indian or am I American?*' rang in my mind. At my core, I was both Jewish *and* American. I understood that duality better now. Being Jewish was my ethnicity, bound up with the terrible history that had shaped my family and so many others like me. It was the color of my eyes, the form of my body, as well as the ancient religion we hold tenaciously as ours even when we don't ascribe to it, while 'American' was my culture and language, my value system and my homeland. I thought of the either/or mentality of Hasidic life and how some of the Hasidim laughed about America as almost a foreign place. The thoughtful among them have their own struggles.

Each side of the hyphen in my hyphenated identity now stood in heightened contrast to one another in a tension that made each side clarify the other. I thought, *This double vision could be a vantage point.* If I'm always a little on the outside yet inside as well, maybe I can better see the whole.

I was in an intimate relationship that was delightfully new, while outside our door, my society was hotly debating our right to marry. Sometimes I shook my head over the controversy and said to my lover, 'Who needs their piece of paper?', and on other days, '*This* is where I've landed?'

Mornings, I woke surprised to find her next to me yet again, the bed still warm with our heat. I would trace the outline of her face in early light and marvel at our beautiful impermanence; I loved that she wasn't tied to me by law or tradition or family expectations. I loved that I had found her there beside me yet again only because she wanted to be there, as was I. *This*, I thought, *is a love marriage*.

A few years passed. The law changed, and we were swept up in the novelty and excitement of broad public support for our union after our years of a private life. We did get married. In a way, I did it for the look of pure vulnerability in her face, suffused with light that spring day in the garden, and the way her eyes went wide with wonder when I said, 'I do.' I was filled with a warm and startled sense of responsibility that tied me to her in a new way.

For years afterwards, I would remember Mythili and Murthy and see again the love and dependence and appreciation I had seen in the faces of those two very different people when they looked at one another. Something ineffable happens when, because of tradition and culture, you let the whole town or the whole country carry you through the streets in wedding celebration straight to your uncharted destiny.

A short time after Mythili and Murthy told me their story, a friend of theirs invited me to an *arangetram,* a coming-of-age dance performance by a fifteen year-old girl. In Tamil, the term means something like 'stepping onto a stage.' The performance seemed to function as a social announcement, like the cotillions of my Southern American youth. "They're using a hall near you," the woman said. "You should come."

"Where?" I said.

"The Jewish Community Center."

Dozens were milling the JCC theater lobby that day balancing little plates of delicacies in their hands, the air pungent with coconut, ginger, tamarind, chai. I had come dressed in artist black only to find the women in brilliant saris; I felt like a crow among peacocks. I settled into a seat in the familiar theater to watch a classic saga about a journey to spiritual enlightenment. A kind man in the next seat warned me that people might sing along.

Curtain, lights down; the story began, sung by a woman in a wandering whining tone against impossibly elaborate rhythms from a tabla drummer who sat cross-legged at the side of the stage. Our American high school girl entered, paused before a flower-bedecked Krishna, and gave a deep bow.

She danced without pause for two hours. It was hypnotic. It seemed her feet were tied to the drumbeat. I was in some ancient temple amid the smell of incense, the drone of the penitent. Her gestures were like ancient Buddha statues, thumb to forefinger with wrist cocked, or a knee raised to the side at an impossible right angle with toes flexed upward. *You are of the past*, the dance, the music whispered. *Live in the dance, in the song.*

I have grown up among you, my people, and with you I will remain, this girl who I imagined spoke English with a mild Texas accent was telling her community. On the last beat, she held a knee up, toes pointed downward, palms together above her head framing her young face and held that impossible pose as the audience rose to their feet with a roar, as they clapped, and wiped their eyes, and clapped still more. Deep in that glowing crowd, I thought, *Assimilation is a lie.*

Once they came to this country, my people felt they had to work on themselves to look and sound like the white majority, as the only way to succeed. We did assimilate, to a certain degree, but that's not a benign thing. We did it out of fear, and need.

As the audience clapped, a wave of demands from adults in my young world bubbled out of my Jewish past: anglicize that name, lose the accent, fix your nose, do something about that wavy hair and be sure to lighten it. Model yourself on a fantasy television world in which color and ethnicity is benign because everyone in the scene sounds the same as the white Christian majority, and they all want the same things, WASP as invincible norm. Several of the Jewish girlfriends of those years had their noses bobbed and their ears pinned at sixteen as a coming-of-age gift from their parents.

As we Jews began to, almost, disappear into the crowd, social clubs and neighborhood covenants that had always excluded Jews, university quotas, restrictions on professional privileges, even a portion of the good old White Boy business network, came tumbling down. With our incidentally white skin, we could fight for and even win a share in the privilege, and then hold on, but we could never quite *be* them.

Around me, the crowd in serious business suits and jewel-like saris clapped in celebration of a young woman whose dance was a promise to all present that she would not forget who she was, even if she, American girl, moved on to make her own choices about life and love.

Then she stepped to the podium and delivered (I swear) a Bat Mitzvah speech: "Thank you, Mom, for driving me to dance lessons like a trillion times, and thank you, Uncle Moorty, for flying in from Poughkeepsie." I slipped out of the hall and drove the short distance to my apartment complex that housed a dozen languages — my home.

Intermezzo

Voices

From Pakistan (arranged marriage):
"I cried, and I locked the door. I called my father and my mother in Pakistan and said, 'Come get me. Come get me!' I would turn on Pakistani music because I was alone. There are no mountains here, and no old, old buildings.

"What changed for me? Time. Having children. I love to garden. And I learned to drive. I made friends. Now I go out when I want. I do what I want.

"My husband helped me so much. Oh, yes, I'm the luckiest person in the world."

From Cuba:
"My father found a job helping to lay steel girders for new highways. My mother mended people's clothes. For Christmas, I asked for a coat. I was never cold in Havana."

From Mexico:
"All the best things in life I found in the US. I tasted my first fried chicken in Houston!"

From the USSR (man):
"The social worker offered me 'sofa,' but 'Sofa' in Russian is a woman's name. She asked me this three, four times. I said, 'Why I want Sofa when I have my wife?'"

From Vietnam:
"When I am older and I have my own home, I want my parents to come and live with me, and I hope my siblings stay close by. It's too easy to let a new culture take over and lose who you are."

From Nigeria:
"People here don't understand the respect you must give your elders, the pride you must bear yourself. That's why I tell everyone to call me 'Mrs.'"

From Pakistan:
"Spanish people have been in Texas for four hundred years, and they still love their language! They are why I only speak Urdu to my baby."

From Mexico:
"In the laundromat across the street, we put in pesos instead of quarters, and it worked!"

From Ukraine, USSR:

"I got here, and they told me to fill out their forms. They said, 'Write down everything about you.' I see 'sex.' I ask them, 'You want to know about that, too?'"

Scene Three

Crusade

It was 1971, and I was fifteen, at an age when think your peers are who you are, when evangelist Billy Graham brought his ten-day Crusade for Christ to Dallas, my hometown. Night after night, a bass-voiced announcer on the evening news filled our living room in a tone of awed respect as the camera panned the crowds in Texas Stadium, a sea of faces awash in gleam-eyed reverence, and it seemed they were all white and all blond and they all had straight hair.

One morning during Graham's Crusade, I skipped school and hopped on a bus downtown to wander and wonder. My city had always been invisible to me in its banality, just as I didn't see our drooping porch or the rusted toys on the stoop as others might see them. The day was clear with an intensely blue sky and a brisk wind off the Texas prairie. I headed downtown as a child, my questions, my stirring discomfort, unformulated.

I got off in the business district in a world of concrete and skyscrapers and honking traffic. I walked, aimless, then stopped at an intersection clogged with cars. Beside me, a woman with a briefcase and sensible shoes.

A policeman wearing sunglasses stood in the middle of the intersection with a whistle in his lips. He held up both hands to hold cars back from all directions and tooted a warning at them, short and sharp. The light changed, and no one moved. The policeman looked over his shoulder, blew the whistle again, and gestured with his chin to a young man at the curb.

The young man was lean and tall with taut, hairy calves and long Jesus-colored hair that hung below his shoulders and blew in the wind. He wore a burlap tunic to his calves tied around his waist with a piece of rope, brown leather sandals, and a crown of plastic thorns. Over his shoulder, he held the crossbar of a rough-cut wooden cross that stretched out far behind him. He stepped off alone into the street.

The policeman held up both hands. All commerce and bustle, all noise of cars and people, had ceased. The world held its breath. I had stepped into a vacuum.

The man leaned hard into his burden, step after measured step, joy and pride and suffering in his face, in his raised chin and beatific expression, in his solemn, tortured pace. He worked so at his terrible, lonely job that I wanted to rush in and help him. The wind ruffled the tunic around his calves.

When he stepped onto the opposite curb, the world woke up. Drivers rolled down their windows and shouted their approval, stuck out their arms and waved their hands in fist pumps of victory, amid a symphony of car horns and two-fingered whistles high and shrill, and it all sounded like applause. Beside me, the woman with the briefcase wiped her eyes.

I was filled with a strange new sense of alienation. It seemed I was not of this city of my birth after all, or of these people who I had thought were mine.

By day, our door stayed unlocked as I burst in and out to school, neighbors, and friends. Every church in my city of churches signed on to help with the Crusade. Thousands of Christian youth fanned out across the city to spread the Word. During that ten-day period, another clean-cut, well-intentioned pair knocked at our door six to eight times a day to flash pamphlets and overconfident too-white smiles, seeking to convert us. Our home was under siege.

If I had to trace the awakening of my religious/ethnic identity to a single moment, it would be the first time that I answered the door to two of Graham's Christian Youth Crusaders, both around my age, come to correct and change me.

Magnetized as I was to identify with my peers, theirs was a clear message: *You need to be like us. Let's fix that.* I was filled with new, angry, ethnic pride.

Perhaps the two young Christians were unaware of what the term 'Crusade' meant to us as Jews. Maybe they knew little about those unpaid rabbles of old who tore into our homes, killed, and raped us, then continued on their way. However, I felt certain Billy Graham knew the implications in the title when he chose it for his campaign. I pointed to the *mezuzah* on our door, mark of a Jewish home, and told the two to go away, but it was too late. My peers at the door had made it clear: I was not one of them. I was not really from here.

I had no idea back then where identity politics could lead my country, the finger pointing and taking of sides, the hardening of differences to the point of violence, just as I didn't yet understand how 'you are not one of us' can chase away a teen still trying to find herself in others. Within the year, I started my spiral into a Jewish version of their fundamentalism and joined one of the few evangelical Jewish groups in history. The message of the Hasidim was too enticing: *We are your truest roots. Among us, you are from here.* I thought I had come home.

I noted this connection, or coincidence, only years later looking back, because that is what memoir does.

Scene Four

Not From Here, Again

I began to follow famous Americans of color with timid admiration. It seemed that to be a person of color in the United States was to live one's defining truth openly, no choice, rather than bearing it as some relic of otherness, scared into blending into white America and bred to forget, like my family. I was still so naïve. I thought people of color couldn't look in the mirror and fool themselves into thinking they were other than who they saw; couldn't detach that face from history and bury their stories in order to gain status in this skewed society and then teach their children to do the same, as my family had done. I missed how inevitable it is to feel you must grapple with a majority-defined "difference" in oneself if it's one you have seen hated by others, missed how very human it is for some to feel compelled to study how to "pass" among the majority in a thousand subtle ways.

I had long felt secretly alienated from America's great struggle with skin color. "We were immigrants," I would say. "We weren't even here" during the foundational persecution of Black people in my country, ignoring the fact that I was formed as a product of my society with its forked perspectives, it's nervous fascination with color. If ours is a whole nation of immigrant families, had others also felt little responsibility for our legacy of shame, for the same reason? Is this part of why we were so mired?

Perhaps to claim America as home was to acknowledge its sins and struggles as my own regardless of when my family came, because history equals past plus present plus future; history is a force that continually shapes all of us through time. That would mean I had an obligation to relate to every individual within the context of both their family/ethnic history *and* American history. Identity plus context.

I guess I was finally becoming an American.

It seemed as if a strange fever infected every American at birth, or upon first setting foot on this land. The fever bred awkwardness, resentment, suspicion, separatism, fear, and even violence about something as innocuous as differences in skin color.

I began to read, like a fiend, filling my mind with voices long overdue in my country, and found a perspective unfairly withheld from me through my formation in white America. Edward Baptist, Annette Gordon-Reed, Isabelle Wilkerson, chief among many. Their brave and patient accounts spoken somehow without rancor did not change my perspective, rather, they gave me perspective, gifted me, centered me, changed me.

And I finally understood that in the United States, 'white' as a status had always been a construct of color plus Christian background, and my Jewish family could only tick one of those boxes. In my country, we Jews were fake white, white by default, always lacking the complacent security that comes with the label, "white" unless the special form of racism against my people peeked out from beneath the surface of time. Maybe that's why I once fled.

Thus began another awakening.

Part Four

A Persecuted Ethnicity

Just Imagine

USSR, 1985

On the day that you apply for an exit visa to leave the United Soviet Socialist Republic, you are fired from your job, and there will be no other work available to you. Word spreads. People point at you on the street. Friends shun you. You know that if your former boss decides to report that you've been privy to state secrets, your application will be refused. You have had no such access to state secrets — your former boss has no basis for such a claim — but that's irrelevant. If he reports that you have had access and blocks your application, he will be honored as a loyal citizen and possibly get a promotion. You know Soviet authorities will interpret his claim any way they choose since virtually everything in the Soviet Union is the State.

If they deny your application, people will call you a *refusenik*, and you will spend the rest of your life scrabbling on the edge. It will be a challenge to afford food. There's the Russian winter.

To survive while you wait, you buy and sell on the black market, where every sale is a risk that you'll be arrested. With an arrest record, you will never be allowed to leave. Mornings, you wake to the uniquely communist shame of reaping profit, capitalist evil.

Months pass, years. You grow numb, so that you cannot, do not, savor any single moment as a last taste of home. You decide to stop waiting and take stock of the wreckage you have made of your life. Then an envelope arrives in the mail.

You are allowed to take one suitcase and enough money to equal what was once one month's pay. You keep your head down on the train.

At the border, the guard calls you a traitor. After your lifetime of indoctrination in Soviet love of country, when the guard adds with a curl in his lip, 'You may never return,' it is as if your mother just said, 'You are no longer my child.' You have always wanted to leave, always craved that elusive quality called freedom, but you can't help it; the guard's words trace a cold line down your spine. As if spitting the words at you, he says, 'This is no longer your home.'

You take a train to Rome with the last of your money.

You arrive to find a representative from the Hebrew Immigrant Aid Society waiting for you holding a sign with your name on it. She offers you a loan to pay for temporary lodging until some country agrees to admit you. You accept gratefully and begin your new life in debt.

Of the one and a half million Jews who will ultimately leave the Soviet Union fleeing twentieth century anti-Semitism, one million will go to tiny Israel, increasing that country's population by twenty percent, but you tell the HIAS representative you want to go to the United States. This is the first time in your life you have been allowed to choose where you live.

You had gained exit from the Soviet Union by producing an invitation from a "relative" in Israel. Before you can apply to live in the United States, you must first formally turn down the invitation from Israel. It's another risky move, but you do it.

You don't speak a word of Italian. You go out and walk for miles, stopping in every storefront, looking for a job that doesn't require you to speak.

Now outside of the collective conscience that was your country, you struggle to imagine what it is, or what it could be, to be a Jew — that title long foisted on you, that old itch you would like to shrug away. Raised as you were in an atheist society, to you being Jewish has little to do with faith. You see yourself as a relic of a people who once carried their peculiar religion around like a banner. It's an old ethnicity in your genes, a fetish of the Soviet government. You don't feel Jewish, whatever that means, unless you replay in your mind your grandmother's Yiddish songs or consider that sense you get of a secret bond of survivors when among other Jews, or the way the outline of the old empty synagogue in town continues to haunt you. Fellow former Soviet Jews laugh at your musings. Better now, they say, to focus on finding a job.

Maybe it doesn't matter being so labeled when you know nothing about Jewish culture in the world. You are free now to drop the association. You can re-invent yourself, change your name, have children who will never face what you have faced, but that unease... You picture the lines in your father's forehead, and the way he looked when he drank. You seem to need to understand this troublesome identity, this enigma that has led to losing everything you know.

The questions remain unanswered through the months at your new job while you wait and hope the United States will accept you. Your days are defined by enforced silence, sweat-stained clothes and aching muscles, that dull fatigue by evening.

Moving to the United States brings another set of challenges. There is little opportunity to muse, and so the questions remain.

In time, you begin to value those questions you never did address, about identity and religion and your purpose in the world. You live as if a question mark is left floating ever before you like an emblem that points the way. You begin to think of that emblem as a key mark of your new freedom, a sign of your new consciousness, shaped by your past. Because you have changed. You now value questions that cannot be answered. You are vigilant about the consequences of any doctrine, and wary of answers that smack of finality. You want to remain open to new ideas and varied opinions and change.

Your Jewish history will keep you aware.

Scene One

Manya, *Kiev, Ukraine, USSR*

For nearly seventy years, the USSR outlawed anything to do with the Jewish religion. That included Jewish gatherings, prayer, ritual items, and literature. They forbade our *language*, sent Jews to frozen Siberian prison camps for decades for owning a single scrap of paper printed in Hebrew or Yiddish. Jewish educational and religious institutions that had developed across the region over hundreds of years, rich repositories of our history and culture, were shuttered, and eventually, forgotten. In the early years of the Soviet Union, police stormed homes, searched belongings, and arrested tens of thousands of Jews. Most never returned.

Everyone in the USSR was required to carry an ID booklet. On the first page were boxes titled 'Name' and 'Nationality.' Russian, Ukrainian, Lithuanian, Estonian, Jew: Jewish was a nationality, but you could only enter one; you could not be, for example, both Ukrainian and Jewish. It didn't matter if generations of your family lay buried near your home, or if you spoke the language as your breath and heart. It didn't matter if you breathed the same air, dressed and ate and behaved in a thousand ways the same as your neighbors, or if you sat with friends in school and sang the same songs, your heart pumped full of the same communist hope and love of the land. You were a Jew, that is, not from here. The proof was right there in your ID.

After Stalin, the labels remained. So did anti-Jewish laws, arrests of Jewish intellectuals, artists, and dissidents, and the gulag. Jews were often blocked from universities, promotions, and party membership. Social slurs were a norm. There were attacks on the street as police looked away. in 1989, after sixty-seven years of Soviet oppression, the United States granted refugee status to Jews from the Soviet Union. This resulted in one of the biggest waves of Jewish immigration in history. Most went to Israel, but half a million former Soviet Jews went to the United States. Manya was one of them.

I swallowed hard at her doorstep. The past had a ferocious pull, a great sucking sound. We had been wives and mothers together. Our children were playmates and schoolmates. I was a pariah in her community now. I knocked. Manya opened the door.

She wore a wig, a long skirt that hung around her calves, and a long-sleeved blouse closed at the neck. There was loss etched in her face; she had been recently bereaved. She murmured a welcome.

The quiet home was dotted with photographs of her husband and children in happier times. She offered me tea, which I declined, then she pulled two dining chairs away from the table for us to sit almost knee-to-knee. A three-legged dog bounded up and settled on her lap. In my mind, my wife stood just behind me with a warm hand on my shoulder.

"I'm grateful you're willing to talk," I said.

"Why wouldn't I?" Manya said.

We both knew why.

"I'm just glad someone wants to hear my story," she said. Then, we were in the Soviet Union with Manya as a school child. It seemed she had struggled for religious freedom from a young age.

"They said in school that there was no God. 'If there was a God,' they said, 'he'd never allow the Russians to go up into space — a powerful ruler like this God would never allow invaders into his territory,' but even as a girl, I thought, *It could be that there is a God.*"

I could see this communist God her teachers described — a broad-shouldered man in military uniform with a raft of Soviet medals on his chest. *How classic*, I thought. *Even communist atheists created God in their own image.*

"I was born in Kyiv, capital of Ukraine. Ukraine became part of the Soviet Union in 1922, well before I was born, but from then until the Second World War, the Russian government still allowed Ukrainian Jews to live their Jewish life, so that my father, who was older than my mother, got to grow up in an openly Jewish household.

Later, he saved his Jewish information in his head since it was too dangerous to write down, but every now and then he sent me outside to make sure no police were around, and when I came back and said, 'Coast is clear,' he told me about his Jewish childhood. He told me how, every week, his mother lit candles and prepared the Sabbath meal, and he told me stories and songs she taught him.

"When I went walking in the city with my mother, I would look at the big old synagogue, but my mother told me not to look, and she rushed me past. She said only old Jewish men who didn't work any more went in there because if you were seen going in, it would be the end of your career or worse. I never once saw the inside. She made sure of that." Manya smiled.

Manya's family lived in a Soviet apartment block assigned them by the government. They went often to visit her father's mother, who had managed long before to get assigned to the old family home, together with Manya's great-uncle. Another family occupied each of the other rooms in that big old house, most of them cousins, and they all shared the kitchen.

"My grandmother and uncle were two of sixteen siblings, but of course, the Nazis came to Kyiv."

Just like that the account slid to a stop. Of sixteen siblings, only the two of them had not been murdered, but then, any Jewish story from that area would have muffled shouts and the sound of shots and shoveling in the background.

Before the Second World War, Ukraine had one of the largest concentrations of Jews in the world. A third of all Ukrainian urban centers were majority Jewish, and in a number of towns, half to three-quarters were Jews.

As the Germans approached, some of them escaped into the Russian interior, right into Stalin's arms. Anyone who managed to straggle back returned to a ghost town emptied of a large part of its populace as over seventy per cent of Ukrainian Jews were dead, including nearly every Jewish person in Kyiv.

Over two days in September of 1941, German soldiers corralled thirty-four thousand Jewish people at a ravine on a riverbank outside of Kyiv called Babi Yar. They ordered their captives to strip naked, jump freefall fifteen feet into the gorge, and lie down on the cold mud in straight tight rows, arms at their sides like toppled toy soldiers lined up for child's play. They shiver, frigid air on bare skin, and the touch of another's skin against theirs will be their last sensations.

Soldiers climb down after them and walk the neat line of warm heads, eyes alive with terror, or soft with resignation. The soldiers lower their muzzles and shoot each person one time in the neck. That day, German soldiers waste, murder, snuff out, slay, erase every individual, every human being, beating heart, pool of stories, each basket of love, trove of loss, a house of irreplaceable knowledge lying before them. Each is a library burned.

A vacuum forms in the world in place of all that each would have given or done or accomplished, and all that their progeny would have given or done or accomplished, stretching into the future in an endless line, leaving a bottomless black hole. Those soldiers shoot each loving, yearning woman, man, girl, boy, and infant lined up at their boots.

A shot, and gone. Repeat. A shot, and gone. Repeat.
A shot, and gone. Repeat. A shot, and gone. Repeat.
A shot, and gone. Repeat. A shot, and gone. Repeat.
A shot, and gone. Repeat. A shot, and gone. Repeat.
A shot, and gone. Repeat. A shot, and gone. Repeat.
A shot, and gone. Repeat. A shot, and gone. Repeat.
A shot, and gone. Repeat. A shot, and gone. Repeat.
A shot, and gone. Repeat. A shot, and gone. Repeat.
A shot, and gone. Repeat. A shot, and gone. Repeat.
A shot, and gone. Repeat. A shot, and gone. Repeat.
A shot, and gone. Repeat. A shot, and gone. Repeat.
A shot, and gone. Repeat. A shot, and gone. Repeat.
A shot, and gone. Repeat. A shot, and gone. Repeat.
A shot, and gone. Repeat. A shot, and gone. Repeat.
A shot, and gone. Repeat. A shot, and gone. Repeat.
A shot, and gone. Repeat. A shot, and gone. Repeat.
A shot, and gone. Repeat. A shot, and gone. Repeat.
A shot, and gone. Repeat. A shot, and gone. Repeat.
A shot, and gone. Repeat. A shot, and gone. Repeat.
A shot, and gone. Repeat. A shot, and gone. Repeat.
A shot, and gone. Repeat. A shot, and gone. Repeat.
A shot, and gone. Repeat. A shot, and gone. Repeat.
A shot, and gone. Repeat. A shot, and gone. Repeat.
A shot, and gone. Repeat. A shot, and gone. Repeat.
A shot, and gone. Repeat. A shot, and gone. Repeat.
A shot, and gone. Repeat. A shot, and gone. Repeat.
A shot, and gone. Repeat. A shot, and gone. Repeat.
A shot, and gone. Repeat. A shot, and gone. Repeat.

A shot, and gone. Repeat. A shot, and gone. Repeat.
A shot, and gone. Repeat. A shot, and gone. Repeat.
A shot, and gone. Repeat. A shot, and gone. Repeat.
A shot, and gone. Repeat. A shot, and gone. Repeat.
A shot, and gone. Repeat. A shot, and gone. Repeat.
A shot, and gone. Repeat. A shot, and gone. Repeat.
A shot, and gone.

Repeat.

They order the second group of adults and children to lie on top of the newly dead at perfect right angles to the first in the same tight, orderly rows, their still-warm heads in a convenient line. A last gift, the lingering heat from the bodies below them is a moment of comfort, of welcome.

The soldiers walk on the bodies of the first group in order to kill this second group more easily.

The pile grows. Over two days, these men who are no longer men, these non-men, nonhumans, these creatures who lost the title of human in the very first act, commit the largest single massacre of the Holocaust.

After Jews, the Germans bring more people to Babi Yar. They continue for weeks. Here they obliterate, end, murder more hearts and minds and useful hands and purposeful feet, more people with gifts and knowledge and needs and hunger. Each person they kill is a keen witness to their crimes.

Each watches them in the act until their final moment.

The Germans bring to Babi Yar homosexuals, communists, prisoners, Romas, the disabled, aged, and ill, members of the resistance, and anyone rumored to have helped Jews, until over one hundred thousand witnesses lie in this place on a foundation of Jewish bodies, the original hated ones.

Manya was born nearby less than five years later. Neighbors and friends and relatives of Manya's family most certainly were buried at Babi Yar. What does that do to a city's soul? How does such a place mark someone growing up nearby? No wonder her father's family clung to their God.

Although I came of age with a Texas accent not far from a horse stable in Dallas, graves of the slaughtered had probably always flickered at the edges of my imagination, a silent gift of my family who left people they loved behind in Europe to be slaughtered and never spoke of them. Then one day, just outside of Houston, a mass grave was found on an old sugar plantation that had continued after slavery by using Black convict labor. The grave contained dozens of skeletons of African-American boys and men chained together. No one seemed to know why they were all killed at once.

Perhaps there is no such thing as leaving.

Then, Manya did what the Soviets did after the war, what every Jewish adult in my childhood always did: she gave her brief nod to the Germans and skimmed past, intent on rescuing her happy childhood from the noise of history and epithet.

"When Passover came, my father took us to my grandmother's house. She baked *matzoh* for us in her oven." Matzoh, a Jewish ritual item for Passover, was expressly forbidden by the Soviets, with a penalty of imprisonment that could be long-term.

"Wait," I said. "No one did that in the Soviet Union! Not innocently. Not easily."

Manya chuckled, clearly proud.

It's a broad flat cracker of flour and water dubbed 'Bread of Affliction' in Jewish tradition, eaten at the Passover ritual meal, traditionally held up as the food ancient Egyptians fed Jewish slaves. When those biblical Jewish slaves fled, it is said they brought their matzoh with them.

To the Hasidim, every bite of matzoh holds a group memory of oppression, and every bite is resonant with escape from tyranny, echoing the escape from Egypt. Matzoh became a promise of escape to freedom. Little wonder the Soviets outlawed it.

"Late on Passover night, before we left her house, my grandmother wrapped matzos she made for us in cloth. My father didn't explain why we took the package or why we carried it home hidden in our coats. He just said, 'This is the time of year we eat matzoh.'

I was a child; I didn't know we were doing anything dangerous. I understood not to ask why. Only when I got older, I heard stories about local Jews who had disappeared, and no one heard from them again — arrested for having something Jewish like matzoh.

"When we got home from my grandmother's house, we didn't make a seder. None of us had been allowed to study anything Jewish for so long that no one could read the Hebrew. Instead, my father told me Jewish stories from his childhood. His stories took the place of a seder. Then, he gave me a bite of matzoh.

"Before that, my great-uncle used to lead a real seder in their house, but everyone was afraid to explain to us children what they were doing. We just waited at the end of the table for food. We knew we could not ask questions."

This densely symbolic, ritualized meal-as-prayer has opened for millennia with children posing questions. The entire service is structured around questions and designed to encourage them. I could not think of a better symbol of oppression than this silencing of a child's curiosity at the seder table.

The Soviets forbade the ritual meal. Perhaps they understood to what extent it is a celebration of freedom. Throughout history, Jews have stubbornly made seders proclaiming their freedom even in the worst of circumstances — there were secret seders at Auschwitz — and they have just as stubbornly reminded one another of past oppression at seders in times of abundance. I thought, *Oh let this work, this opera, this book, be a seder — a sumptuous meal shaped by memory, celebrating American freedom. Let our freedom be bright.* It was my first prayer in years.

The dog jumped down from Manya's lap. There was the sound of lapping water from a bowl on the kitchen floor. Manya's face softened when he returned. There was a little rebellion in her love of him since Hasidim frown on owning non-kosher animals, especially dogs. He jumped on her lap.

Manya's grandmother's house seemed to glow for her in memory. She returned there again and again, this time to describe her great-uncle coming home on Yom Kippur from the synagogue — the one Manya was cautioned not to look at and had never entered. The extended family joined the uncle as he broke his fast in yet another meal the children accepted without explanation and knew not to ask why. Manya also mentioned triangular pastries her grandmother made on Purim (a holiday, she found only later, that celebrates a time when Jews averted a holocaust), and the fried potato pancakes her grandmother made for Hanukkah, a holiday that also celebrates surviving religious persecution. "For us, everything Jewish was food related. We knew nothing of the stories behind the holidays, and we knew nothing about God," and yet, the child Manya absorbed the way those secret family gatherings implied a mysterious God no one dared define.

I had come to her home hoping for a recounting of school, neighbors, her mother, had hoped for an inside portrait of the life and dreams of a Soviet girl, but to Manya, these occasional secret Jewish encounters scattered through her childhood were glimmers that pointed out her path to her present life, her path to God.

"After we married, we had a problem because we had gotten our invitations from Israel separately, before we met. Only an invitation as a couple would mean we would get to leave the country together, if they let us go at all."

In 1963, a movement to free Soviet Jews began in the United States that grew over twenty years until massive rallies were held around the world that were widely covered in the media. The image-conscious Soviets were embarrassed. To save face, they opened the door in their tightly closed border, for Jews only. Thousands rushed to apply to leave, even though they knew that a completed application was an incriminating document, written proof of disloyalty.

Many of the first applicants were sent to Siberia. Then the Soviets closed the door, but that sparked more public protests around the world. They opened it again, again only for Jews. Still more applied. The startled Soviets announced that applicants would now only be eligible to go to Israel, and they were required to produce a letter of invitation from an Israeli relative. Israeli 'cousins' quickly materialized.

This is the process to which Manya referred. If she and her husband filed separate invitations from Israeli 'relatives,' the government might release the two of them years apart or only allow one of them to leave. They decided to write to Israel for a new, single invitation addressed to them both as a unit. If one was denied exit, the other would stay behind, too. They would reapply until they could leave together.

They had not yet applied for an exit visa, which is why they still had jobs.

"We started the process all over again. Then, emigration closed. We thought it was closed for ever."

Manya's husband finished his medical training. They were assigned by the government to a remote village. I assumed the unfortunate posting had something to do with the fact that they were Jews. Medical equipment in the village was scarce. There were wood stoves, and outhouses in the snow.

They lived in the village for three years. Then Manya became pregnant. She wanted to give birth in a city hospital. She wanted her mother, but in the Soviet Union, citizens were required to apply for a permit for internal travel. Manya put in the request, and the Soviets allowed the couple to go to Kyiv for the birth.

After the birth, Manya didn't want to return and raise their child in the village. That wasn't her only worry.

"The whole time I was pregnant, I was afraid I was going to have a boy. I knew my husband would want to circumcise our son, and I knew he would ignore the danger if we did, but to me, circumcision was barbaric. Why would you do that to a baby?

"It turned out to be a girl. I was very happy."

They petitioned to remain in Kyiv even though doing so was an audacious and possibly career-threatening request. Permission was granted.

"Our son was born two years later. I told my husband I didn't want to circumcise him, but he looked into it anyway. His father found someone who agreed to do it — someone in Moscow."

They did not have a travel permit to go to Moscow, and they couldn't apply for one for such a mission. Her husband was undeterred.

Moscow is nearly five hundred miles from Kyiv. That meant officially thirteen hours by train, and delays could make the journey interminable. To travel such a distance with a newborn and without a permit, to the seat of government in a world filled with spies, authorities checking papers at every stop, to go intent on meeting a secret mohel for an illegal procedure...

Manya's husband scheduled the circumcision. Then Manya fell ill and couldn't travel. Once she was better, the baby contracted a urinary infection. They never went.

"Were you relieved?" I said.

She smiled. "I didn't mind."

They received a joint invitation from Israel.

Manya had been listing her miracles, every one of them deemed nearly impossible: permission to remain in Kyiv without damaging her husband's career, delay of the circumcision, as if the delay was a promise that the right time would come, and now a joint invitation. They quickly applied to the government for exit visas, and they were completely surprised to receive paperwork and permits within a few weeks. Another of her miracles. Most waited years, and there were always consequences of applying such as losing their jobs. Many were refused exit.

Manya said goodbye to her mother.

At the border, the guard confiscated their passports. They were now officially stateless.

The little family took a train from the border to Vienna, with Rome one of two cities that offered to Soviet Jewish refugees temporary residence. Once there, Manya and her husband scrambled for minimal housing, work in a language they did not speak, and food. They applied for US refugee status. Then, months of uncertainty.

Manya's description of arriving in the States was striking for what she did not say. There was none of the expansiveness, the joy I heard from other former Soviet refugees. She didn't marvel that they could now choose where to live, or that she could travel wherever she wished in the country without a permit. She expressed no surprise at people living on the street that the government did not house, did not marvel at the piles of produce in the grocery store. I wondered if she had ever really arrived.

When I used to enter Hasidic homes, as soon as the door shut behind me, I would fall into a kind of casual intimacy as if a familiar skin had just closed around us. Each of those homes had the same Hebrew books lined on the shelves, the same religious art, and always a photograph of the Rebbe on the wall. Inside that home, the contentions of the secular world with its godlessness, its violence, and pessimism, its foreignness, fell away. We became a country unto ourselves with our own interests, and our own language peppered with Hebrew and Yiddish phrases.

I had fallen back into that country and that language with Manya, as if, inside her home with her three-legged dog, neither of us was quite in America.

Once the US granted refugee status to Soviet Jews, Jewish organizations across the country raised funds to sponsor them. Jewish Family Services, a United Way social services agency, did the same. Manya and her family had no relatives or friends in Houston. They had no contacts at all. Jewish Family Services provided them with an apartment, furniture, three months' rent, and offered to help them find jobs.

"Almost as soon as we got here, we talked about a circumcision for our son. My husband wanted this very much, but we were one of the first Russian-speaking families to come to Houston; we barely spoke English, and we had no one to guide us. We didn't know how to find a mohel. We decided to ask a doctor to do it."

The boy was no longer an infant; the procedure would have to be done in a hospital.

The family still needed to enroll the children in school, find a means of transportation, find work, and master the language. Using a checking account was new to them, and coming as they did from a communist society, so was paying rent, insurance, and taxes. Yet, thousands of male Soviet Jewish refugees had themselves and their sons circumcised right after they arrived, just to gain that mark in the flesh that has always been a defiant, "This is who I am." I thought, *Identity is a mystery.*

"We found a Houston doctor and asked him to do the circumcision. Instead, he referred us to Rabbi P, a mohel who was fluent in Russian. This made us very happy. We allowed the rabbi to do the circumcision. It was clean and fast, and our son suffered no pain."

Manya was deeply grateful that the procedure was safe and legal, and not the one she'd managed to avoid after her son's birth, the one that had made me think of backroom abortions.

"Our daughter was now seven. We sent her to the local public school, but very soon it seemed like a waste of time. She already knew everything they taught her, and she kept bringing home homework about people we didn't understand, like Martin Luther King. Black people were very strange to us. What did Martin Luther King have to do with us?"

I blinked. Manya had been in the United States for years at this point, yet it seemed she still didn't see how the story of a man who dared speak out against oppression of a long-beleaguered class related to her, just as she didn't seem to see landing in a country with Martin Luther King Day as a national holiday as a reassuring sign, at least of the country's ideals. Neither did she seem to take reassurance from the way this country holds onto King's memory as a way to hold ourselves accountable. She expressed her question of years before as if it was still viable.

'What did Martin Luther King have to do with us?'

What *did* he have to do with us, as Jews, or as Americans? Only everything.

"Rabbi P invited us to his home for a Sabbath meal and we went. That night, there was another Russian-speaking guest there named Viktor who talked a lot about the Hasidic school. He wanted us to put our kids in the school. He even offered to pay."

With no previous exposure to capitalism or religion, raised in a society that provided housing at no cost, Manya did not note that she had just been offered gifts that are never free. When I first met Hasidim working in outreach, I also missed the signs.

"We went to see the school, but we did not consider it for our children. A Russian friend told us, 'At that school, they pray all morning until lunchtime, and when their brains are dead, they learn a little.'

"We were afraid of them. These people seemed like nerds. They wore beards and long black coats like in the seventeenth century.

"A few weeks later, Viktor invited us to his house for their son's birthday party. There we saw Jewish children in obviously Jewish clothing playing and calling each other Jewish names. They were so open!"

Manya stood for a while and watched the children, the most vulnerable of her people, dressed openly as Jews, labeled openly as Jews, playing freely without fear. She took this as a powerful statement of religious freedom in her adopted country. "We decided we had to give the school a try. In a short time, we saw that our kids were happy. They made friends. We decided to keep them in the school.

"Little by little, we developed a close relationship with those people. I never felt pressure from them. They were welcoming, and the classes they invited me to made me feel good. I began to believe what they believed. It took a long time, but I became one of them. They became our home."

The dog was asleep in Manya's lap.

I thought back over what I knew of her communist childhood, and of Binh's — of children afraid to ask questions, forbidden all but a few dreams of their own. I remembered my own kids in the same school as Manya's reciting by rote pages and pages of prayers and assertions of faith with only glimmers of the freedom of mind Ali had equated with America, and yet, I knew I had come into this interview with a certain arrogance. I had been convinced that in joining the Hasidim, Manya had simply given up one form of totalitarianism for another. Now I understood that Hasidic life crystallized for Manya exactly what she had sought all along — the freedom to practice her religion without consequence or danger, even if she used that freedom to immerse herself in a group that demanded she sacrifice a good portion of her freedom as a woman, a group that held itself apart from the varied cacophony we called America. It was a *choice*. Manya knew going in how that life would restrict her. She chose to equate the Hasidic form of Judaism with her very identity and saw exercising that choice in her adopted country as her truest freedom.

All over the United States were people who willingly embraced strict versions of their religion and forfeited control over much of their lives in the process. The freedom of religion embedded in the US Constitution allowed people to choose to limit their freedom. Maybe that was a paradox of democracy.

Then there was this: the same freedom of choice had allowed me to reject religious rule over my life. Manya and I didn't stand so far apart after all.

At the door I took an impulsive step forward to open my lesbian arms to my former compatriot, mother of my children's beloved playmates... and stopped myself. I thanked her again and said goodbye.

My last image was of Manya in the doorway with the dog in her arms. As I walked away over a rolling green lawn dotted with fallen leaves, the sky open to infinite possibilities, I realized the silent roiling backdrop to Manya's story; ranks of Hasidic emissaries from our same evangelical group had moved in secret across the USSR throughout Manya's childhood. They smuggled Jewish texts to clandestine basement yeshivas; they brought prayerbooks to furtive prayer groups that met in a different place every time and then melted away; they wound forbidden phylacteries on men, smuggled Sabbath candles to women, brought groups matzoh and taught them how to conduct secret Passover seders.

Rabbi P was born in Russia among those secret religious Jews. He once told me of a childhood trapdoor beneath a neighbor's living room rug that led down a dark dank stairway to a hidden mikvah ritual bath. He spoke of a handwritten notebook kept inside another book on his father's shelf that listed forbidden circumcisions that his father, a secret mohel, had performed. If Manya's husband had managed to have their son circumcised before they left, they might have met Rabbi P's father.

Rabbi P was the mohel for three of my sons. Each of those circumcision ceremonies for my boys was a festive, public affair, the boy and his Jewish soul welcomed by the men amid clapping and song.

There was a point after leaving the Hasidim that I offered one of my sons my abject apology for making a permanent mark on the most private, precious part of his body before he was old enough to have a say in the matter. "It's your body. It should have been your choice," I moaned. My son was an adult by then, but young enough to blush, and scoff at my regret.

Once home in the quirky little place that I shared with my wife, I shook my head. Jews were once contemporaries of Amorites and Assyrians. I didn't know why we were still a distinct people, but Jewish culture had come to ask us to sacrifice for the sake of preserving Jewish identity, beginning in infancy. I still couldn't say that I ascribed to this, but historically, in our culture and in Manya, I saw something proud and fierce that just might have hinted as to why, in part, we had survived.

In 1991, two years after the United States granted Soviet Jews refugee status, the USSR collapsed. The United States almost immediately rescinded the status, but Jews never stopped leaving the region. Since the Soviets first opened the door, nearly five million Jews have poured out of what was their homeland. In the same period of time that began with Soviet collapse, Jews have been expelled from the other large old Jewish communities that survived the Holocaust, in North Africa and the Middle East. By 2022, half of the world's Jewish population was in the United States.

Months after Manya's interview, I tried to imagine the music for the Russian Jewish movement. There were the Yiddish songs behind closed doors, but to let those songs sing out loud didn't seem true to the stories. No, this music had a strangled voice overwhelmed by all things Russian. I called Chris, the composer. "No klezmer," I said. "No Jewish-sounding clarinet."

"What are you thinking?" he said.

"Giant chords. Shostakovich. Soviet boots stomping on piano keys."

"Got it," he said, this brilliant man.

In the end, the orchestra dominated the movement with huge dissonance and great clashing brass. Against that backdrop, individual voices built on one another to tell a defiant story of Jewish survival.

Intermezzo

Voices

From the USSR (Holocaust survivor brought to the US as an old man):
"The street is very steep, and it is covered with ice. They make us shovel sand to make the way easy for their trucks. They stand over us with guns — that is what I remember — and then trucks begin to pass filled with people in them. They are going away from the building where they first gathered us. I count the trucks: one, two, three, four. From the fifth truck, I hear my mother scream. 'Malkiel!'

"I don't look up. I keep shoveling.

"I never saw her again.

"Later, my friend put me on his shoulders and helped me climb over the fence around the ghetto. He promised he would follow. There was barbed wire, five rows. My pants got caught, but I got them off and jumped down and ran to hide in some bushes. I hid until the patrol passed. They passed very close.

"I waited a long time. My friend never came.

"It's not that survivors' stories are so miraculous — it's that they're the only ones you get to hear. How do you stay alive three years in a forest? You learn to be the animal that you are.

"When the Russian Army came, they knew animals make good soldiers.

"They made me a Soviet soldier, then, a good communist worker, husband, father — anything but a Jew.

"My daughter brought me here, an old man. She brought me because, in the end, that is what I am: a Jew."

From Russia, USSR:
"Every Jew knew his limits."

From Ukraine, USSR, post-glasnost:
"We came home from shopping — me, my dad, and my mom. We were outside our apartment building, and we heard shots. It was our neighbor shooting at us from a window high above us.

"We screamed and tried to hide behind a bush. We held each other. My father tried to cover me with his body. Bullets hit the dirt right next to me. I was twelve. Of course, the police did nothing. We were Jews."

From the USSR:
"My husband knew French, Italian, and English; he looked for work as a translator, but every job, he'd call, and they'd say, 'Yes, the job is available.' Then, when he went there and showed his ID, they said, 'Oh, you're Jewish. That job is filled.'"

From Ukraine, USSR:
"He was bigger than me. He held me backwards over a hot stove with his hand up over my face and screamed, 'You Jew! You are all Russia's problems.'"

From Chechnya, USSR:
"The Muslim majority in our town protected us Jews during the Second World War. We got along. Plus, we looked alike."

From Chechnya, USSR:
"I was a pediatrician, twenty-five years. Then all around us, there were kidnappings — three Jewish neighbors, all friends. We had to leave."

Another from Chechnya, USSR (now in college studying comparative religion):
"I was thirteen when we came to the United States. The Jewish community gave us an apartment, and they sent me to a Jewish school, but we studied religion there. Religion! What was a God? What

was prayer? I knew the names of a few of the holidays, and I didn't eat pork; I was proud to be a Jew, but the idea of religion was very strange to me."

From Russia, USSR:
"In the hard times after immigration, I thought, *My parent's lives were so difficult; why should I think I deserve more?* Then I decided, maybe this way I can give a better life to my children."

From Ukraine, USSR:
"At forty-seven, I had a Bar Mitzvah. The Houston Chronicle had an article about it. I didn't do it because I believe; the communists took that away from us. I did it to show those Soviet bastards that there's something they can't take away from me: I am a Jew."

From Pakistan:
"In my town, there was a mosque on every corner. Everyone prayed. It was the law; you had no choice. You didn't think about it. After I came to the US, I became a wild boy; so much beer, and girls.

I'm older now. To me, America is all about family and religion, but in this country you do religion to feel good about yourself and not because you have to."

Scene Two

Elias and Susannah with their adult children: Samuel, Abigail, Marcus, and Luke, *Rivers State, Nigeria*
(Absent: siblings Anthony and Estelle)

I had become a walking jangle of ghosts, a collection of stones from everywhere. The project had grown far beyond the opera, beyond the question of identity — of who I was, or who anyone was, or who I am now — and beyond waking from the dream. A scrim had been pulled away from life and world, and another, and another, until history and our destruction beyond borders and faces from around the globe came alive and colored even my most banal of visions, as if I could see across time without camouflage. I was haunted by questions: *Could I be responsible for this world I inhabit? Was I more so as an artist?* I thought, *But all I can do is look.*

And listen. I could listen.

The Ogoni people have lived for over two thousand years in southeastern Nigeria on four hundred square miles of the fertile Niger Delta. For most of their history, the soil was rich, harvests were abundant, and in this many-rivered state, fishing was a rich resource. Over the centuries, the Ogoni lived in clusters and because of this developed five distinct languages and as many dialects, but all continued to identify themselves as Ogoni.

In my mind, a camera pans the landscape. It zooms in on children at play, and on mothers stirring huge pots of sumptuous stews over an outdoor flame. Fishermen haul in straining nets. Farmers gather their heaps, sweating torsos sleek and muscular and strong.

In 1958, Royal Dutch Shell found enormous oil deposits beneath Ogoniland. They struck an agreement with the Nigerian Government and began drilling that year.

If Shell happened to find oil under, for example, the public thoroughfare that runs in front of my home in Houston, they would strike a contract with the City of Houston and not with me; I'd have no choice about the drilling, and I would reap no benefit. If Shell wanted to drill just a few feet north on my private property, they could do so only with my formal agreement by contract. Going forward, they would be required to rent the land from me for an agreed-upon amount. If I also happened to own the mineral rights to my land, Shell would have to pay me a share of the profits from whatever they extracted in perpetuity. Later, if Shell inserted a new pipeline that happened to burst and leak into my soil so that my garden and our majestic Texas ash, home to bees and squirrels and jays in spring, withered and died, if the oil continued to leak until our home was moored on a field of black mud slick and viscous, if oil leeched into our pipes so that water from my faucet poured out cloudy and stank and sickened us, if it leaked and sank into the water table deep below the surface and sickened everyone in the area, Shell would be held liable for cleanup and have to do so under Federal supervision. They would be required to pay damages to health and property to everyone who suffered.

The United States holds its industries responsible for the environment with the Clean Air Act, the Oil Pollution Act, the Safe Drinking Water Act, the Comprehensive Environmental Response Act, the Compensation and Liability Act, and many others. The problem is, the legislation applies only to industry activity within US borders.

Over two million Ogoni still live in what is now Rivers State, Nigeria, also known as Ogoniland. When Shell first arrived, their lucrative agreement with the Nigerian Government didn't mention the people who held claim to the land. The agreement did not provide for any Ogoni compensation, or for a share in the profits from what they would extract.

The Nigerian Government must have expected the Ogoni to object, because they sent armed militia to guard as Shell drilled into Ogoni family fields, and as they laid four-foot-tall pipelines above ground through the center of Ogoni villages and across family thresholds. They shot anyone who dared protest. An alarm sounded through the area. *Say nothing or die.*

Then, the pipes deteriorated. Oil began to leak. Precious dirt turned black and viscous. Entire rivers stank with it, still pools covered with a rainbow sheen. Crops dwindled. Fish died.

A noxious odor rose from water and ground that permeated the air, food, clothing, hair. Gas leaks formed dark clouds that hovered over family fields.

Rather than build facilities to recapture the gas during the extraction process, as they do now, Shell set the leaks on fire. Ogoniland became a hellish landscape in paradise. Columns of flame leapt skyward from the ground with a constant roar. There was a frequent enormous BOOM every time another pocket of gas escaped.

A twentieth century version of colonialism had come to Nigeria. Instead of the British Crown, corporate interest partnered with a corrupt Nigerian government now stole Ogoni property and lives. Worse, this time they were destroying the land.

The problem was, this was oil, and Black Africa. Around the world, people averted their eyes.

I was beginning to understand that I lived in a great golden magnet that feeds this level of greed around the world. Then, as now, half of Nigerian oil went to the US market.

With no option, Ogoni people ate the blackened produce, drank the stinking water, and grew ill. Children were born and faded. The death rate soared. The land and its people were perpetually dying. Ogoniland is still the most polluted place in the world.

The essence of the Ogoni story is about water. I had never thought twice about the flush of a toilet or about taking a shower; never felt the need to drink from a stream; never experienced thirst that set off an adrenaline rush of fear. In all Ogoniland, there was no clean water and not a single water treatment plant. Women walked miles to buy and haul home a single bottle of clean water. They still do.

I am a Houstonian. My city is home to the world headquarters of several major players in the oil industry; I am open-eyed about the ubiquity of oil, and I understand the depth of our dependence.

I am aware as well of our fragility because of that dependence.

In the US, thousands of miles of underground pipelines are laid underground across the country that converge on the Port of Houston. An oil field east of where I live stretches over a significant portion of Texas, Louisiana, and the Gulf of Mexico. West of my home is the Permian Basin, one of the world's most productive fracking fields.

Twenty-five per cent of my state's water is used for fracking.

There have been destructive leaks from those underground pipelines all over my country. Entire communities have been poisoned by corporate indifference, their ground and air tainted with benzene. Leaks are followed with a great deal of finger pointing, fines, and uneven compliance.

Houston is located on the fertile Gulf Coast where it never snows, where there are two full growing seasons a year; the land around my city produces a great deal of food for the region, and the warm Gulf waters teem with oysters, shrimp, flounder, and trout. Corrupt our government just a little more, neglect the aging pipelines, back off a little farther from poor supervision, or close an eye altogether on compliance — it wouldn't take much for the Gulf Coast to become Ogoniland.

Then came an Ogoni man named Ken Saro-Wiwa. He was a novelist and a former professor of African literature. He had produced a popular sitcom, which meant his face was familiar throughout the country. Saro-Wiwa got himself elected to the Rivers State legislature. Once in, he stood up before the Assembly and argued passionately for Ogoni autonomy.

Rivers State was (and still is) a rich source of income for Nigeria. The council forced him to withdraw from the legislature. That dismissal became a fabled part of Ken Saro-Wiwa's story. It is often retold, in proud Nigeria, to illustrate how Saro-Wiwa was willing to face condemnation in public by the ruling body for the Ogoni cause.

Ogoni elders soon met and together formed MOSOP, the Movement for the Survival of the Ogoni People. Elias, father of the family I had come to meet, was one of those elders, although I didn't yet know. They decided to ask popular, visible Ken Saro-Wiwa to lead. He would be the public face for the cause.

Ken Saro-Wiwa stepped into his new role with all the bearing and purpose of a Nigerian warrior. His voice would be his spear.

I knew nothing of this history when I first met Luke, youngest son of Elias. Luke was a soccer friend of another subject, in one of those lively immigrant leagues like the cricket club that once connected Ali to his fortune. "You have to hear Luke's story," the young man had told me. I took his word for it.

I met Luke in a diner soon after. He was gangly and lean, and a little too polite in a nice young man kind of way. We took a booth and ordered, but Luke ate little. He said the food in this country didn't seem healthy. He looked down and pushed at crumbs on the table as he spoke. "My family — we're all citizens now. Me, I finished high school; I got a scholarship to a college in Kansas."

"Well?" I asked.

He finally looked up, then held his gaze long enough for me to register an objection. "I didn't stay," he said.

The mother in me kicked in. "You still have to make a life for yourself," I said. He was such a nice young man.

"It's my mother," Luke said. He sat up as if to change the subject. "You have to meet my family!"

I wasn't ready to let go. "And you?" I said.

Luke pushed at a few more crumbs. "I don't know how I can leave her," he said.

Then we were in Luke's parents' place where his siblings, all adults, had come together for our meeting. It was a brick suburban home in one of the many outlying Houston neighborhoods that were filled with newcomers. Here was Luke looking happy, bouncing on his heels as he introduced his father — tall, serious Elias — and Susannah, his diminutive mother whom he couldn't leave, and his older siblings, Samuel, Abigail, and Marcus.

Each greeted me in turn, then as everyone was talking at once, Marcus turned to make sure his mother sat down first. We settled on a comfortably worn, brown sofa and unmatched chairs.

Susannah seemed queenly yet vulnerable in her colorful turban on her armchair throne. She looked to her husband and then to each of her children. She was supervising them or seeking reassurance, I wasn't sure which. Then, all eyes were on Elias. Someone cracked a joke, and suddenly Samuel, Abigail, Marcus, and Luke began to tease their father with gentle jabs as if chiding him that he still held himself solemn leader of his clan. I cleared my throat.

I thanked them for coming together from their various homes and families. I knew that Marcus had several children, and Abigail had a son. I was there, I said, to hear them tell me about how they got here. "Luke said your story is really something," I said.

"Oh, yes," Abigail said, and there were nods around the room.

Elias frowned. There was his skeptical gaze, his formal demeanor. He narrowed his eyes. "Can you write whatever we say here?" he said. He spoke slowly, and his voice was rich and round and mellifluous. Baritone, I thought.

Then, far into this project, I realized that not one of the people I'd listened to before Elias had asked if I was free to write whatever they told me. What did he imagine might hold me back? I thought of Luisa who feared her own freedom to speak with good reason but had trusted my freedom to write. Meanwhile, , still new to current American society, I had found that personal information was no longer personal; personal information had become public fodder.

I wonder today why Elias' query didn't give me pause at that time when memories of the censoring Hasidim were still fresh. I had first started to write while living among them and during that formative time felt their silencing authority over what I wrote like a leash and jerk on my collar, but that day with the Ogoni family, I was still reveling in my new freedom, and still idealized it. "You can tell me anything," I assured Elias. "I can write whatever I want."

There was that gaze again.

Then, he began.

"In the early 1950s, our Ogoni economy was buoyant. We farmed, and we had good harvests.

We did fishing, and we always had a good catch. Then Royal Dutch Shell came to Nigeria. By 1990, the devastation from oil was too much. Cropland soaked with it ran for miles. Oil got in the food as it grew. There was oil on our own family land, but we could not get money for it."

Elias was describing his own childhood in idyllic pre-oil days. He was a boy when Shell arrived, then spent his coming-of-age watching his homeland progressively poisoned. Everything he had been trained to do was becoming futile and slipping away.

"You know, I used to be hungry all the time," Luke said. He was jumping us forward by decades, into his own childhood in Ogoniland. "Whenever I did get food, I ate it standing up in a hurry because you were hungry, and you might not get more for a long time."

My boys as teens dash into the kitchen from basketball, breathless, hair sweat-tousled. They grab food at random and eat on their feet, as if their eating right now is urgent.

"What did you eat?" I asked.

"Garri. That's made from cassava," Samuel said.

"Cassava is a white root," Susannah, their mother, said. "I soaked it for maybe an hour and washed it until it got soft. Then I washed it some more." She and Abigail both laughed, remembering such drawn out work for a simple meal, remembering it here in the States where slow food is fast compared to preparing cassava.

"It's a lo-o-ong process," Abigail said. "The result is a hot cereal, and it's worth the wait, but a person can stay hungry a long time until it's ready."

"You plant the stick, and it yields a kind of root — the part we call cassava," Elias, the farmer, said.

The conversation quickened with memories of food in hungry days so that (I couldn't help it) I thought of Holocaust memoirs that told of starving people in camp bunkers trading sumptuous recipes far into the night. I thought of the fanciful cookbook compiled in Theresienstadt that had been published after its authors had been killed. I had a copy, but reading it disturbed me so that I didn't know why I kept it.

Garri is a white, cooked mush that is eaten all over the African continent. The cereal is poor in nutrients and contains a trace of arsenic, but filling and high in carbohydrates; it is a perfect base for anyone whose days revolve around physical labor. I've found African recipes in which garri is enriched by topping it with milk and chunks of coconut and peanuts, or mixed with ground nuts, or used to thicken meat soups. Garri can be cooked with beans, or prepared with honey and fruit. It can be dried and ground into flour, then mixed with water to form a dough and baked into fufu balls that are then dipped by hand into sauces or stew, dip and bite. Finding this array of recipes for garri across Africa heightened for me this family's picture of Ogoni poverty, where a single unadorned dish of garri was an unreliable luxury.

"Garri was our most basic food," Elias said, "but the cassava wouldn't grow. It wouldn't grow! We planted it anyway, but if it didn't die, it came up deformed and black."

Here was Elias in the field, sun in his eyes, holding a withered plant from which hangs a shrunken blackened tuber. He looks toward his home, his family.

"Do you ever wish you could go back to Nigeria?" I said. I knew it was a ridiculous, even audacious, question, but I had developed a strange desire for the hostile landscape my grandparents once fled. Wanting that proverbial home was a baseline inheritance, a yearning for something I couldn't define; I wanted the centering, the connection to my history, that had been cut off. Some people can't ever go back, and a rootlessness wends through their family into the present day.

A phantom-limb feeling had been implanted in me. Could my home ever become that unearthed and shrunken tuber? Could a day come when I had to leave my country, as my family once had to do?

I knew that flickering unease as intrinsic to my Jewish consciousness, part of an inheritance of a thousand years of displacement.

If I ever had to leave, no matter how hostile the environment had become, I would still yearn at times to go back.

The room erupted at my question.

"Go back? What? Oh, no. Not me. No. No way. Seriously?"

"You have to understand," Luke said. "Smoke and fire came out of the ground like it was normal. You saw black clouds of gas sitting on the fields that grew your food, and always that horrible hissing sound."

"Living in Ogoniland is living in hell," Elias said with a frown. "Smoke full of chemicals fills our air and covers our skin. It covers what we grow. You eat it. You drink it."

"Everyone was sick all the time," Susannah said.

Then I realized: only Elias was speaking in the present tense, as if he alone still imagined himself in Nigeria.

"Would you like water?" Abigail said. She went off to the kitchen and came back with a pitcher full, and tumblers.

Susannah's dark eyes flickered. "You have to understand! Fish die over there," she said. "You're sick all the time from the water and the air, and you're starving. You fall from the load on your head. You lie there and wait for hours for help, but there's nobody with the strength to lift you up. People fell and died like that every day, so many we couldn't keep track. Died for no reason."

"I had many friends who died from this oil disease," Marcus said. "I mean, you were trapped in it." Marcus was talking about his childhood.

"There was one school for many villages. You could walk three hours each way to school," Abigail said. "Some of my friends walked home, and come Monday, they didn't show up in class, and then my parents would tell me why."

"I mean," Samuel said, "I see my friend in school, and someone passes me a note that says he has the oil sickness, so then I know it's just a matter of time. When he doesn't show up a few days later, I shrug my shoulders."

He was trying to sound nonchalant.

"You shrugged at your friend dying?" I said.

"You had to," Abigail said. "It was oh so common."

"Or face your own death," Marcus said.

"Well, we all faced that," Samuel said. "Death is nothing we were scared of. You got used to it. I could be at a funeral and hear that another person died, and I'd just think, Oh, dang, now I have to go to another funeral."

"Yeah, we got used to it," Abigail said. She looked like she had tasted a lemon.

"Really," Luke said. "Dying isn't taken serious that much over there. I mean, I see someone one day, and then I don't. You get to feel like, okay, don't get attached to anyone. It happened to my best friend! I told him one day, 'Stop by in the morning, and we'll walk to school together,' and then, walking home that day, he just died."

I thought, just, no. Luke was twelve years old when they left Nigeria. When I was twelve, my friends were my soul. I thought of the space and quiet one needs to be able to grieve. I had never thought it a privilege to get to regret a death or feel a loss. "This," said Samuel, "is starvation."

Then Elias countered his children's words, gentle but firm, as if insisting their more human feelings were always there. He didn't seem to like their bravado, refused to shrug at the daily deaths in Ogoniland. Maybe this alone was proof that Elias could lead. "The truth is, in Ogoniland you live in fear," he said. Abigail, Samuel, Marcus, and Luke looked down. "Very few of Ogoni children live to adulthood," he said. "There are no hospitals in Ogoniland. Death can meet you anywhere. You die like something without value."

As if Elias had re-opened a path to real feeling in his adult children, as if Samuel, Abigail, Marcus, and Luke suddenly remembered that it was okay now in well-fed safety to have feelings and to miss their dead neighbors and even laugh, remembering them., everyone started talking at once about friends who had died, *Remember her? Remember him?* shifting almost seamlessly from the numb denial of their childhood into felt loss, acceptance, and love.

There was something I had to ask Susannah. "When you have kids," I said, "all you want is to protect them, but you were in Ogoniland — how did you keep all of your children alive?"

Susannah looked shocked. "How did I keep them alive? It wasn't me!" she said. "There was nothing I could do. It is God's grace that we are alive!" She grew quiet. "Over there, when you're pregnant, you can't be happy. How to keep my children alive? The only thing was to hope in God."

"That hope," Luke said, shaking his head. "My dad was always preaching, 'Better days are coming.' He told us all the time, 'We will have good times again.' You hear that every day, it becomes your backbone."

"That was the difference between us and other families," Abigail said.

"Our dad told us all the time that we were like the Children of Israel, except the Children of Israel went through harder times than we were going through," Marcus said.

"We started every day with, Dad says it'll get better," Samuel said.

"The kids that didn't have parents telling them that better days were coming... they felt hopeless, Luke said. "They gave up."

"God loves the Ogoni people," Elias said, "and He is active among us. By His grace, we are alive. This is what drove us. We had to make the government see."

I wondered how Elias and the other Ogoni leaders even thought that a corrupt and faceless government could be awakened to Ogoni humanity. I knew from years in the Hasidic world that when you embody inconvenient truth, you can be the one who gets sacrificed. I thought, *Elias had the illogical kind of courage that can bring change*, but I corrected myself. Elias would call that courage 'faith.'

"We Ogoni elders found powerful leadership in the writer Ken Saro-Wiwa," Elias said. "We met with him; then we petitioned the Nigerian Government to give the Ogoni our share in the oil. We wrote an Ogoni Bill of Rights and sent that to the government as well. We signed the Bill of Rights with our names."

I thought of all the people who were shot by Nigerian military for protesting the drilling. I had spent half of my life hiding from the cruel world.

"That... was a dangerous thing to do," I said.

Elias leveled a look at me.

Just as Elias wouldn't call what he did courageous, he also wouldn't call it hope. To him, faith was not a feeling or a commitment; faith was action.

Ken Saro-Wiwa, an admirer of Mahatma Gandhi, began to travel and speak in churches all over Ogoniland. Wherever he went, he urged people to prepare for non-violent protest. He also publicized Ogoni's plight throughout Great Britain, home of Royal Dutch Shell, and beseeched the world to help heal the land.

Saro-Wiwa appointed Elias head of the new Ogoni Council of Churches. Elias became spiritual leader of the movement.

"Without my father, there would be no movement," Abigail said. "The spiritual struggle *is* the struggle."

Abigail had just equated her father with spiritual struggle. The movement, the fight to survive, faith, her father, were all one.

"Ogoni are religious people," Elias said. "We wanted God to guide our leadership." The churches would be their megaphone.

Soon, Ogoni clergy across the region were preaching non-violent resistance and leading congregants in prayer for MOSOP, the new movement. Saro-Wiwa gained huge popular support. Across Ogoniland, there was new hope.

As the oldest sibling present that day, Samuel took on the part of emcee. "Ken Saro-Wiwa led our fight," he said with a note of proper awe in his voice. "He had been outside of the country for years before this, studying at Oxford and becoming a writer."

"He lived in London and won a prestigious award for his writing," Luke said.

"He published all over the world," Samuel said, "but then he came home to lead our people and get important organizations outside of Nigeria to pay attention to our suffering."

Actually, Ken Saro-Wiwa earned his PhD the University of Ibadan, a respected Nigerian university, but he never won a literary award that I could find, and he never studied at Oxford. However, both Saro-Wiwa's role model, Mahatma Gandhi, and Saro-Wiwa's son, Ken Wiwa, Jr., had lived in England (never at Oxford) and Ken Wiwa, Jr., later won the prestigious Hurston/Wright Legacy Award for his memoir about his father.

Samuel and Luke had rolled Ken Saro-Wiwa, Mahatma Gandhi, and Ken Wiwa, Jr. into one great mythic leader.

I thought of the Hasidim, hounded from country to country, of how tenaciously they held to myths about their past leaders. Each set of stories about a leader was shared like a shared lifeline of hope. It seemed that facts had little to do with what a myth has to offer.

The day came when a group of Ogoni landowners gathered at a drill site and peacefully obstructed the operations. Within twenty-four hours, Nigerian military poured into Ogoniland. They shot anyone they thought might interfere with the work.

"A neighbor who was our friend tried to stand guard over her field where she grew the food for her family," Samuel said. "She raised her arm up to stop them, and they shot her arm off."

The following was published years later by Amnesty International after a court allowed Amnesty International to review thousands of internal Shell documents from the place and time referred to above:

"Evidence shows that Shell repeatedly encouraged Nigerian military to deal with the protests, with full knowledge that this would lead to unlawful killings, rape, torture, and burning of villages. Shell provided the Nigerian military with material support and transport, and in at least one instance paid a military commander who was notorious for human rights violations."[2]

In January of 1993, after thirty-five years of oil extraction from Ogoniland, Ken Saro-Wiwa led a march of over 300,000 Ogoni through four urban centers. The very next morning, Nigerian soldiers occupied 27 Ogoni townships. The soldiers were members of a military branch that Nigeria had formed to use against its own people called the Nigerian Mobile Police, or MOPOL. That day, the Mobile Police shot and killed two thousand Ogoni people. They burned homes. They left 80,000 people homeless.

The boot remained on Ogoniland.

"Every night, we heard shooting, and in the morning, we found out who they killed," Samuel said.

---

[2] *"In the Dock: Shell's complicity in the arbitrary execution of the Ogoni Nine,"* posted on amnesty.org June 29, 1997 https://www.amnesty.org/en/documents/afr44/6604/2017/en/

"Soldiers raided our house and stole our things so many times that we had nothing left. The place was an empty box," Abigail said.

"I had a few friends they shot in the chest," Luke said. Luke was nine at the time.

Susannah said, "You could be in the market buying food for your family, and if they'd been looking for someone and didn't find him and found you there, they'd shoot you instead. I saw soldiers kill people in the market for nothing."

"They raped a lot of us," Abigail said. "Girls stopped going to school. No place was safe. Two years I didn't go to school. I couldn't step outside." Abigail was fifteen and sixteen during this time.

"No school for any of us," Marcus said. He was twelve and thirteen.

Every face around the room was hot with memories.

"It's not like American soldiers," Samuel said. "American soldiers, the government sends them out and gives them food and money and a place to stay, but these soldiers, they are handed guns and told they don't have a choice, even though they aren't given money or food. They want to survive, and they're desperate, so, if one of them needs to shoot someone so he can eat…"

"They have to take care of themselves," Abigail said.

"You're a soldier, you have a gun, who's gonna stop you?" Luke said.

"No one can fight back," Abigail said.

"You're justified by your uniform," Samuel said.

There was a pause.

The Mobile Police was hunting everyone connected with Ogoni resistance. Elias had gone into hiding. Most nights, soldiers pounded on the door after midnight.

"They'd be yelling, 'Where is your father? Where is he? WHERE IS HE?'" Abigail said.

"We had to answer the door," Samuel said.

One look at Samuel, and I decided he knew, as did the family down to the youngest, that each time they answered the door, that moment might be their last.

"It was tougher than before," Abigail said. "We barely ate. Mom went to work every day, but they never paid her. The military hunted anyone working with MOSOP. Dad was in hiding, schools shut, us kids stuck inside, hungry, nowhere to go. No one to help us. No one dared even visit or they'd get implicated," she said.

"Sometimes Dad slipped into the house in the middle of the night to check on us. He woke us up to talk with us. That gave us strength," Samuel said.

"How did you know when to run away again?" I said.

"It was the sound of their trucks," Luke said. "When the people hear a military truck, they run, and yell, and you run, too. You don't ask questions."

I could hear the ululations across Nigeria.

"Everyone yells. That alerts people for miles," Marcus said.

"Anyway, our friends always warned us when they saw trucks coming," Abigail said, "and then my dad would be gone."

"A truckload of soldiers might come at midnight," Elias said, "but by the time they got to our door, someone had already alerted me, and I'd go."

Samuel laughed. "It got so that anytime Dad was home and we heard a truck, we'd laugh," he said.

"You laughed?"

Now everyone was laughing.

"Yeah!" Abigail said. "Just when our dad ran out the back door, we'd yell, 'Better not forget your shaving kit. If they catch you, you won't get to come back for it!'"

I had never seen faith like the faith in this family. I didn't think they had ever pretended to one another that their faith would keep them safe from the Mobile Police or guarantee that Elias would live another day after he dashed out the door. It didn't seem they had ever denied what could happen, and yet they continued to believe that their life, as it was, was part of God's good plan. This peculiar, open eyed, honest faith without delusions, faith humbled before reality, fed their astonishing equanimity. Their faith had formed a solid wall around them and glued them together into a unit, ready for what could come. I could not fathom it.

"It's not true that we all survived," Luke said. "Our grandmother died."

"Oh, I'm sorry," I said.

The room filled with talk about her. *Remember how she always...*

Susannah looked accusingly at Elias, as if an old disappointment, one thread of anger, had finally peeked through the façade. "If my husband hadn't kept running away, my mother would still be alive," she said. "He used to go get medicine for her."

"Well," Elias said. "People were generally sick..."

The siblings objected. "Grandmother should have lived. She wasn't even seventy!"

"Our grandmother was tough," Samuel said. "When soldiers came to the door, she would get so angry, she didn't care what she told them."

Abigail laughed out loud. "One time, a military man came to the door, and our grandmother picked up her walking stick and waved it at him! She told him if he came again, she was going to poke him!" Then, they were laughing about using a walking stick against such power and the little woman who brandished it.

I thought, *So, the grandmother's strength led them as well.*

Samuel spoke over the others.

"The Mobile Police bothered my grandmother about MOSOP like they did the rest of us, but my grandmother got sick in her heart about our people. It was heavy on her."

"It was tense at my grandmother's funeral," Marcus said.

"Soldiers came looking for me there," Elias said. "They expected me to go to bury her."

"That's right!" Susannah said. "They even came to my mother's funeral."

"You went to the funeral?" I said to Elias.

"Of course, I went," Elias said. "Then someone alerted me, and I slipped out."

"In the beginning," Luke said, "whenever we opened the door and found soldiers were there, they would just say, 'We're looking for your father. Oh, he's not here? Okay'. Then, after a few weeks of us saying, 'We don't know where he is,' they started threatening us. Well, we knew what they'd done to other people, you know, so why not us?"

Many months passed like this, uneasy sleep, the deep thump in the night on the door, the family clustered inside the door with the knowledge that in the next moment any of them could be arrested, or beaten, raped or killed.

"It got worse. The military cordoned off our home," Luke said. "I was ten. I lost all my friends. They were afraid to be seen around me."

"The military came and set up camp in the empty high school behind our house just so they could keep watch on us night and day. They were waiting for our dad," Samuel said. "Then one day, they came to the door and took our mother away."

My heart jumped.

No one spoke. Susannah's silence was huge. Her face was a mask. I thought it possible she had never told her family what the military did to her after that arrest. Even these years later as I write this, her silence that day pulsates on the page.

Later, I would learn that the military arrested Susannah five times. They would keep her for days or weeks, then release her and send her home, perhaps hoping she would be a decoy for Elias.

Their mother in prison, their grandmother dead, their father in hiding, the children lived alone in a looted empty house. Some nights in the small hours, Elias crept in the back door and woke the children with whispered words of assurance and a loving touch for each. He brought them together to hold hands and pray for Susannah. Sometimes he stayed until morning.

"We sent Luke to the prison to bring my wife food," Elias said.

My mind screamed. *You sent a boy to a prison in that system?* Then I wondered what I would have done if I were Elias facing impossible choices. Would I risk my child to keep Susannah alive? Or not?

"Luke was small for his age," Elias said. "We thought, they'll see a child bringing food to his mother and have mercy.

"Luke took her food every day. Each time he went, he walked seven miles."

Here is Luke, a malnourished hungry boy carrying a package of food down an endless hot road, hoping to save his mother.

"Luke spoke English well," Elias said.

English is the lingua franca in Nigeria, this nation of over five hundred languages.

"The guards became familiar with the boy. After a while, they felt free with him," Elias said.

"The head officer even took me to meet his family," Luke said. He sounded proud. "One time, I brought the head officer a letter from my dad. In it, my dad wrote, 'This is an Ogoni struggle. A spiritual struggle.' The guy read the letter; then he started screaming and threatening me. He accused my father of every crazy thing you can think of. I tried to tell him, 'Look, my dad's no monster,' but he screamed, 'Shut up.'"

A handwritten letter was proof Elias was nearby and in touch with his family. I wondered how he justified using his son to play cat and mouse with the military. Regardless, Luke stood up to that dangerous man. I thought, *Luke, this will mark you, and guide you, that you spoke truth to power at such a young age.*

"Soldiers camped at the school for months," Samuel said. "I made friends with one of them. We used to play soccer. One day while we were playing, the soldier told me that what his commanders had told him about my family was not exactly what he saw, watching us. He wanted to know what was really going on, and I told him. I said we just wanted our people to not be sick or hungry. I said my father was spiritual leader."

Samuel was seventeen. They were just two teens pushed too soon into manhood, playing soccer.

"We got close. We became friends, but I knew what I was doing. I made him think he could trust me, but I told my dad everything. Then one day, the soldier told me, 'Look, the government sent me to monitor your dad. If I have to take him out, I will. That's what they told me to do.'"

On May 21, 1994, while Ken Saro-Wiwa was out of the country stumping for the Ogoni cause, four Ogoni leaders, publicly known advocates of non-violence, were found murdered.

Rifts had developed in Ogoni leadership. Some of them had argued passionately for armed resistance, yet Luke was derisive about any suspicion that they might have killed their opponents who were against violence.

"The four who were found murdered?" he said. "It had to be the Nigerian Government who did it. It's obvious that the government killed those four; then they accused Ken Saro-Wiwa of murdering them, as if Ken Saro-Wiwa would have killed his own people, the people he was proud of and wanted to help!"

It does seem intentional that there was never any government investigation. Instead, Nigerian police were waiting for Saro-Wiwa upon his return. They arrested him at the airport. They then arrested eight of the remaining leaders of MOSOP and charged all nine with the murders. The prisoners became the fated Ogoni Nine.

Only Elias remained at large.

"Ken Saro-Wiwa wrote a letter from his jail cell to the world dedicating the Ogoni struggle to my father," Samuel said. "After that letter, there was no way my dad wouldn't continue to speak out."

"I evaded the military for a long time," Elias said. "Then one day, I received a letter from Ken Saro-Wiwa, from jail. He asked me to come meet with him in the military camp where he and the other eight were detained. He wrote that the Nigerian Government wanted to talk about solutions for the Ogoni. He said the Nigerians had asked him to recommend someone who wasn't a prisoner to deliberate on behalf of our people. It was clear to me that Saro-Wiwa believed them because he had given them my name."

I suddenly felt as if I was watching a movie for which I already knew the ending, that Elias would survive, yet I wanted to stand up in the crowded theater and yell at the screen, "Don't go!" It must have shown on my face. The family looked quite amused.

"He had to go," Samuel said. "Or they'd just come get him."

"Your father knew how to get away!" I said. I wondered if Elias' devotion to Saro-Wiwa, and to the Ogoni cause, to God, had blinded him.

Their chuckling sounded comfortable, familiar, as if they had turned this story over between them many times until it softened and lost its bite, or until it broke open and made it clear that this story is how they became who they are.

Perhaps that happens once a story becomes a family myth. Then, details become relative, and the story can grow even larger than reality. I thought, *Sometimes, people justly become, well, mythic.*

"I dressed in my best robes," Elias said. "One of our ministers drove me to the military camp where Ken Saro-Wiwa was being held."

I was still shocked at Elias' determination to go. Around the room, there were outright guffaws.

"Do you know what's really funny?" Samuel said. He was barely able to get the words out. "That very morning…"

"We knew," Abigail said. "We said!"

"We told him. Everybody told him," Luke said.

"We had a feeling this could be the last time we'd see him for a long time, or ever," Abigail said, "and still…"

The king in his finest robes strides into battle.

"I'd gotten away many times before this, oh yes," Elias said.

"Yes, yes!" Abigail said. "Always a step ahead."

"One step ahead!" Luke said.

"He'd been a hunted guy for so long," Abigail said.

"We knew we couldn't trust those people!" Samuel said. "We even tried to send Marcus with him so he could come back and tell us where they were holding our dad, because we knew they would keep him, and that way we could find out what happened!"

"Did Marcus go?" I said, a little worried.

"Our dad would not allow it," Samuel said.

Elias would risk his child for his wife, but he wouldn't allow the same for himself. I wondered, *Is this what tenderness for one's spouse looks like in a ruthless world?*

Abigail laughed. "If we ever got to see our dad, it was quick, at night; then he'd run away. After maybe a year like that, he gets dressed up in robes and walks right into their office!"

"That's the only way they would have gotten him," Susannah said, and her voice sounded as if Elias was Daniel walking into the lions' den, as if he was her Biblical hero. Then, as if chastising her children, she said, "If we didn't believe Ken Saro-Wiwa, what did we have?"

"We arrived, and we asked to see the commander," Elias said.

Elias and his unnamed minister had come expecting to speak as equals with the commander. They were escorted into an interior office and told to sit; they remained under armed guard.

The commander strolled in. He paused, glared at them, and ordered the guard to put Elias and the minister into a cell.

"I was certain the commander was making a mistake. I still believed the letter was from Ken Saro-Wiwa," Elias said. "Even as the guards walked us to the cell, I was still thinking they wanted us to come to negotiate. I couldn't take it in."

Here's the jail cell, with a ragged hungry clutch of unwashed men crouched on a filthy floor. Elias stopped still. "I said to the guard, 'We are not these people,'" Elias said. "The guard said, 'I have orders to take you to detention.' I said, 'We came to meet with the commander.'"

The guard took a threatening step, waved the gun at them, and pointed them into the cell.

"We didn't sit. We stood."

I didn't expect the inmates were too impressed with that.

I was there with Elias, the smell of unwashed bodies, brown floor, clothing brown with dirt, brown faces lined and gaunt and expressionless.

"The prisoners asked why we were there," he said. "We told them, 'We came for a meeting,' and they said, 'Oh, you've been deceived.'"

"You've been deceived!" Susannah said, in the same tone she might use to call out 'Amen!' in church.

"We continued to stand," Elias said. "After an hour or more, the guard came and took us back to the commander's office.

"The commander walked back and forth in front of us and shouted, 'You stand up before Ogoni congregations and tell God to destroy Nigeria! You tell them Nigerian leadership is the devil!' I cleared my throat to talk, and he screamed, 'I am not here to trade words with you!' I said, 'We are here to...' but he yelled, 'Go!' We were immediately surrounded, and they took us back to the cell."

"Back again!" Susannah said.

At the sound of Susannah's voice, I knew that this story of Elias' single imprisonment was so revered in this family, they would repeat it for generations.

Susannah never did speak of her five imprisonments. Not a word.

The moment came when Elias sank to the floor and became just a prisoner among prisoners, when he, too, was overcome with hunger and dirt and basic needs. Two weeks passed. Elias didn't know if he would ever see daylight again. He would not address how he was treated in the jail.

A 2015 plaintiff document filed against Shell Oil by the nephew of Ken Sar-Wiwa describes Elias' imprisonment. Elias was denied food and basic sanitation. He was beaten daily. In this telling before his family, this laying out of his legacy as a leader and a proud man who had suffered for a holy cause, Elias omitted these indignities.

"They had been holding the Ogoni leadership for almost a year," Samuel said. "Now, they had our dad. After he was in jail about two weeks, the Nigerian Government hanged Ken Saro-Wiwa and the other leaders. They hanged all nine of them in one day."

Around the room, the solemn news, the dashing of impossible hope, was fresh again.

I name the Ogoni Nine here, killed for oil by the Nigerian government:

Ken Saro-Wiwa
Saturday Dobee
Nordu Eawo

Daniel Gbooko
Paul Levera
Felix Nuate
Baribor Bera
Barinem Kiobel
John Kpuine

The Nigerians did it for American money.

The day after the hangings, guards moved Elias to a secret location and put him in solitary confinement. "No food. No light. Nothing," Abigail said.

I thought of studies of sensory deprivation, of disturbed sleep, hallucinations, madness.

There was an international outcry. England, the United States, and South Africa recalled their ambassadors. The Commonwealth of Nations expelled Nigeria from among them. The International Monetary Fund denied Nigeria a major loan for oil exploration.

Ogoni spies went to work. They located Elias and arranged to get food to him. Someone on the inside would see that he received a package.

"We brought our dad food," Samuel said, "but we could only hand it to a guard two miles down the road and hope the package got to him."

Elias didn't say if he received the food; his face had grown as stoic as his wife's. Neither did he speculate as to why the Nigerian Government didn't hang him with the others. Now the Nigerians had missed their chance, and the eyes of the world were on them. Elias would say it was God's plan.

One day, a guard came and took Elias out of the cell. I pictured this tall gaunt man in a tattered robe, his walk stiff and halting, squinting in the light. "The guard took me outside and said, 'Just, go!'" Elias said. "Then he said, 'We will hunt you, and we will find you, and when we do, we will kill you, and no one will ever know what happened to you. *That* will be the end of you and your people.'"

Every face in the room had changed. Luke had become a boy in an upside-down world on a hot seven-mile trek to keep his mother alive. Abigail had become a boisterous hidden girl growing into adulthood under the constant threat of rape. Elias, unbowed under his responsibilities, had become a dirty ex-prisoner blinking in the sunlight.

"When I woke the morning they hanged Ken Saro-Wiwa, I felt it was a very big day," Susannah said. "I didn't know what had happened. We got up and went to church." Mother and children filed into a pew. Fellow members nodded in solemn acknowledgement of absent Elias. "Then someone came running into the church and announced that all of the Ogoni leaders had been killed," Susannah said. "I said to myself, *My husband, too?* Everyone jumped up and went outside."

Susannah began to cry. "Outside, people are running, and yelling. Shouting. We stand there in shock. I think, *Where is my husband? Where is he?* Who can we ask?

"One of the people running in the street yells at us. He yells, 'They are saying Ken Saro-Wiwa killed the others!' That's when I knew it was true that the government had killed Ken Saro-Wiwa."

She felt all along that they wanted to kill him and claim it was justified, and now her fear was proven. Worse, the lie that Saro-Wiwa could possibly be a murderer was so blatant, Susannah understood there was no more hope.

"Then I heard one of them yelling my husband's name." Susannah cried out, "When I heard my husband's name, I didn't know what to do. I didn't know what to do!"

She had been through military occupation, her friends and neighbors killed by gunshot or dead of the oil disease, her mother's untimely death, and her children starving. She'd survived home invasions and threats at gunpoint *for years*, the beloved land sick and dying. She'd been imprisoned five times and probably beaten or even raped while she was held. She knew her husband was in solitary confinement. All of this she could endure, but not the possibility that Elias was dead. She could endure all of it only as long as she still had her husband.

I saw Elias' tenderness for Susannah in turn and thought again about what that meant in a brutal world.

"We went back into church," Susannah said. "The church was empty; people were afraid to stay inside because the Mobile Police targeted the places where we gathered. My son held me and held me. He said, 'Shhh, don't cry, be still.' Then. someone came in and told us that my husband had been taken to a different prison. He was alive."

Elias soon found his way home to his family. Given the love and honor and connection between the people I met that day, I could only imagine the reunion.

"Well," Abigail said, "the Ogoni people didn't fight after that. After you lose your leaders, you calm yourself. You think about what happened. You've been humbled. You sit back and ask why."

"Judges from the All-Africa Conference of Churches came from Nairobi to Ogoniland," Elias said. "The World Council of Churches also came."

"A very serious thing," Abigail said.

"I appeared before them and explained everything I have told you here. The World Council asked me to come to their international convention in Brazil to talk about Ogoni."

"Spies would follow you," I said.

"Of course," Elias said.

"Even to the convention in Brazil," I said.

"Yes," Elias said. "I left for Brazil that night."

"I went from Nigeria into Ghana and flew from there to Brazil. I was in Brazil five or six days; I told the Council everything. As soon I got back to Nigeria, I got word that the Mobile Police had new orders to kill me wherever they found me, and they would also kill my family. I couldn't go home. I had to get word to my family.

"I sent a letter through people who would not arouse suspicion, who were unrelated to me. I wrote, 'This time is for real. If you hear military trucks, leave immediately. They will hurt you and possibly kill you. Get out of the country. Go to the refugee camp in Benin. I will find you there.'"

Benin shares Nigeria's western border.

"Then I went to Benin and waited. I remained in hiding."

"I was at home with Samuel when my dad's letter came," Abigail said. "We read it together."

"It must have been hard to imagine your father telling you to forget the Ogoni mission and leave forever," I said. "Also, now *you* were the targets."

"Without the letter, we wouldn't have understood things were any different," Luke said. "The military used to show up every night. They never threatened us kids."

"Military trucks came very soon after we got the letter. As soon as we heard them, me and Luke jumped on the next bus," Marcus said. "Ogoni people hid us along the way."

That escort out of the country was an Ogoni goodbye. Luke and Marcus were twelve and fourteen.

"Why didn't the rest of you go?" I asked.

"Our mother refused to leave," Samuel said.

"Me and Samuel… we had to stay to protect her," Abigail said.

"Why didn't you leave?" I asked Susannah.

"Someone had to protect our property!"

Teenaged Samuel and Abigail stay to protect their mother from murderous soldiers. Their grandmother waves a walking stick at armed gunmen at the door. Now Susannah was ready to stand up to guns to protect her property. It was all as natural as rain.

Susannah shook her head. "When we heard the trucks, I told Samuel and Abigail not to stay. I told them to go. I told them those soldiers were hunting their father, but if they saw the kids, they would hurt them. We knew that now."

The trucks came... and went away.

"Well, my dad was gone, and Luke and Marcus had run off to the refugee camp, so then it was easy. All you had to do was stay where you were, and if more soldiers came to the door, it would be the truth that they found," Abigail said.

Easy, I thought. *Just tell the truth and accept the consequences.* It had taken me so many years to stop hiding from the truth, to live it and accept the fallout.

"We stayed to look after our mother," Abigail said. "We were okay — Samuel and me stayed out of the house most of the time. By six a.m., we'd be out there on alert."

"Then one night, I came home, and I found the house was empty. I went inside to protect it," Susannah said.

"It was a Sunday night, nine o'clock," Abigail said. "Me and Samuel were out back. We heard *bom bom* on the door. We heard voices saying, 'We're looking for Pastor Miller.' Then my mother said, 'I'm sorry. He's not around.'

"'You've been saying that a long time!' They pushed past our mom and went in.

"We peeked around front. There was a whole bunch of jeeps and over fifty soldiers there besides the two guys that went inside."

"I told Abigail to get away fast," Samuel said.

Always the threat of rape. Abigail looked at him and took off. She made it to relatives in another town, where she stayed until Elias sent her safe escort.

Now alone, Samuel looked again through the back window and saw guns. Earlier that day, he had escorted two UN inspectors around the town and he knew they were still around. Samuel ran and found one of them and brought him back to the house. Approaching from behind the house, the two crept up to the window.

Susannah took over telling the story:

"The soldiers walked all around in the house. One of them started yelling, 'Where is the money?' I said, 'Nobody sent money.' He said they would take all our things, and if he found any connection to MOSOP, he'd take me away forever this time.

"I believed him. I sat down on a chair. While they looked all through the house, I closed my eyes and started to pray. They were angry that they didn't find anything.

"One of the soldiers came and stood over me, but I didn't stop praying. He said, 'You are praying against our government!'" Susannah's voice became defiant. "I said, 'I am praying for peace.'" "He said, 'You are praying against Nigeria!' I said, 'I love Nigeria!' He said, 'Shut up,' and I said, 'You shut up!'

"I stood up in front of him and told him again to shut up, then I walked away into the parlor. I sat down there and began to pray some more, but he followed me. He stood over me and said, 'You are praying God will smite me!' I said, 'No, I am not.'" Then he pulled out his *koboko*, [this is a short whip of many tails that can be particularly painful] and he hit me. Beat me."

Susannah's voice was starting to break. "I yelled, 'No. No!' He said, 'You say 'no' again, and I'll hit you more.' He really beat me. I was yelling 'Stop!' and I fell to the floor, but he didn't stop. He hit me and hit me. Then, I was far away somewhere. I could hear myself crying. I could hear him yelling, 'You are weak! Your people are weak!' I saw his boot rise up near my eyes to kick me again... and I didn't know myself anymore."

Outside in back, there was sudden silence from the house. Samuel and the UN inspector looked at one another.

"The screaming stopped," Samuel said. "We heard the front door slam, and we heard the jeeps drive away." Then, more quietly: "We ran inside the house and looked through it for my mother. We ran out the front door and found her unconscious on the step. She must have crawled out there for help." Susannah would not remember doing so. "The UN guy drove us to the hospital."

Elias had said there were no hospitals in Ogoniland. The drive must have taken hours, with Samuel in the back seat trying to tend to his mother, feeling helpless, hoping, praying she would live. In my mind, I heard his mother saying, "There was nothing *I* could do to keep my children alive." All Samuel could do was hope in God.

"To this day, I can't find that UN guy. I wish I could. I want to thank him," Samuel said.

Susannah's kidneys were badly damaged. She had many lacerations and multiple broken bones. She remained in the hospital for some time.

I couldn't speak. I wanted my daughters to meet this daughter of a woman whose voice was her walking stick, this woman who time and again spoke up and stood up to power with full knowledge of what the consequences could be, until this last terrible test. I wanted my daughters to see what impossible courage looked like, and to know that Susannah was here, in our country, in our city, that she was part of us.

Posted online six years after I met this family:

'Dear Ogoni People,
It is with a broken heart that I write to inform the Ogoni people, friends, and well-wishers, of the death of my beloved mother, Susannah, today, after a protracted illness, in Houston, Texas. I will forever miss her love, care, and affection. May her gentle soul rest in the bosom of the Lord who she served throughout her lifetime. The family will keep everyone informed of funeral arrangements. Anthony D.'

The quiet hero of this story, Susannah's last victory was that she did not die of her injuries.

"After that guy beat up my mother, I complained to my friend, the soldier at the high school," Samuel said. "He said, 'Sorry, we're here to do a job.'"

With a sly grin, Abigail pointed at her father. "He caused all this," she said.

As official head of the Ogoni Youth Federation, the oldest sibling Anthony had his own story of persecution and escape. He had also been forced to run away and was in the Benin refugee camp when Luke and Marcus got there. Anthony took his brothers to his tent and looked after them in the camp.

"It was strange getting used to the refugee camp," Luke said. "We only got food once a week, and there was no way what they gave us could last even half that time. We learned fast how to sell it and buy stuff that would keep, like beans and grains."

This is true in refugee camps the world over.

"There was one toilet for thousands of people," Marcus said. "Sounds impossible, but the people organized, and you know, we made it work."

"We only left the camp in groups," Luke said, "so I felt pretty safe, even though there were spies and kidnappings and killings. Plus, my people eat snakes, but some of the others thought snakes were holy, so there were fights over that."

"It's just… we didn't know where our parents were. I worried all the time if they were alive," Luke said. Then, I was back in the diner meeting Luke for the first time, new meaning in his words and in my First World nudging that he should leave his family and return to college as some relevant rite of passage. His incredulous response that day was another that would come to haunt me. *But how can I leave her?*

"Sometimes in the camp, we got letters from our dad, so we knew he was alive," Marcus said.

"Those letters kept me going," Luke said. "That and soccer. I played soccer every day."

"Then, Anthony was sent to the United States," Marcus said. He had no choice. He had to leave."

The US had granted Anthony refugee status. The organization that handled his case sent him to another of the top five American cities where resettlement organizations place new refugees.

The boys were now alone in the camp. Elias was in hiding nearby, but the boys didn't know this at the time; they didn't know where their father's letters were coming from. "Then my father came because he wanted to see us, and the guard refused to let him in!" Luke said.

Elias smiled. "I waited at the gate while the guard went to search for them," he said.

Exposed. I could only imagine the danger.

"The guard found me on the soccer field," Luke said. "I yelled for Marcus. Everyone stopped watching the game to watch us running to the gate! A lot of people ran after us. There was a whole crowd behind us, yelling and cheering. Me and Marcus jumped up onto the gate — it was high. We climbed up and over it and other people climbed up just to watch." Luke dropped onto the ground and launched into his father. "I held him and cried a long time," he said.

"We were in the camp about a year," Marcus said. "Still no school for us."

"I had secured a place with the Jesuits nearby," Elias revealed. "I was safe there for the time being. Then I got an interview at the UN refugee office. The interviewer listened to my situation and gave me emergency refugee status. Then, she reached into her own pocket and handed me money to smuggle the rest of my family out of Nigeria."

The Ogoni network went to work one last time on the family's behalf. Members collected Abigail and Susannah and passed them like precious jewels from person to person until the two were over the border.

The family was together again in Benin. YMCA International flew them to Houston, home of Shell Oil headquarters for the northern hemisphere.

It was towards sunset. I looked around the room, from face to face, everyone healthy, alive, fully present. We were here now. "It has been fifteen years," Elias said. "We have all become citizens. Our children are grown and educated. We own this home."

"And Ogoniland?"

"I go back every year. I continue the work to help my people. I go officially as an American tourist. The military is no longer occupying the area. There's democracy there now, somewhat."

There were groans.

"As US citizens, when we go to Nigeria now, it's just a vacation," Elias said. "We work for improvement so we can go home for good and live among our people."

"The land is just as polluted," Susannah said. "The Ogoni still suffer."

"The Nigerian Government does nothing," Samuel said.

Elias nodded. "Ogoni are starving. They are sick."

"Most of the people who were fighting when we were there were either killed or they left and went to the United States," Abigail said. "The ones who are still there, they don't have the boldness to fight any more."

"There's an elected government in Nigeria now. They no longer molest members of organizations," Elias said. "The people feel free to…"

"They're sicker than before!" Abigail said.

"There is no clean water," Susannah said.

Elias persisted as spokesperson for his family, as if his family was still of one mind. "We feel okay here, but our mind remains back there."

"You can go back. Not me," Marcus said.

"My parents can retire over there if they want; I'm not going back," Luke said.

"It's too hard over there," Abigail said.

I turned to Elias. "How do you manage to help your people now?"

"Mostly, we work from here," Elias said. "MOSOP meets regularly. We contact organizations, and we continue to petition the Nigerian Government."

Who was Elias' 'we?' Had he assembled a virtual network of activists? It was not his family; not any more.

The family had grown quiet out of respect and love for their father and his endless task, but no one echoed Elias as if they were in church. No one invoked Ken Saro-Wiwa's name as if he had been a prophet, not even Susannah. Elias seemed alone in his work now.

"There's no improvement in Ogoniland. None," Susannah said. "I would go visit, but stay there? No. This is my home now." *Susannah stands in the doorway refusing to leave their home in Ogoniland.* I heard the same stubbornness now. Elias looked disappointed, resigned. .

Abigail's voice softened. "I might consider going back if the environment got better," she said, "but the economy would have to be good, too." She folded her arms for emphasis.

"I'd go only if there's peace," Marcus said.

"If there's war…" Susannah said.

"You can never predict war!" Samuel said.

"I don't like war," Susannah said.

No, I thought, *I don't like war.*

"Nobody likes war." Elias' voice had dropped, low and wise with finality.

There passed a single beat of time, of memory, faces and eyes around me full of reflected images from their collective past…and then, they suddenly all began to laugh. I couldn't tell who started it. I wondered if they had all been on the verge. Maybe they laughed because they *could* laugh now, in their adopted home, at something like an understatement about war, and because they still had their good humor, their long-honed weapon against all that could have pulled them down.

Elias finally spoke in the first person, for himself.

"Could it ever feel like home for me in Houston? My children were so young when we came here that they're part American, but where is *my* home? How do I balance a need for safety against my mission in life? My people need me; they look to me for help. I don't feel comfortable that I left them. I can't bear that. If there's never any change over there, it means our struggle was for nothing.

"Yes, I will go back to Africa, even if my family stays here, and I will continue to work for change. It's safe in America, but I cannot bear to continue living in two places. I cannot."

"America lets you come and even become part of the government!" Samuel said.

"I can run for Congress!" Luke said. "All I have to do is get signatures and get my name on a ballot, and who knows, I could even defeat the incumbent. You can't do that in Nigeria."

"We are free here," Abigail said.

Around the room, eyes shone with immigrant love of this country of safety, abundant food, shelter, and clean water, where each person present had found reliable work that paid them with more than promises, a country where people had a voice, and where soldiers didn't storm homes or shoot people in the marketplace.

"You feel you can make a difference here," Abigail said. "In America, it's always, let's work together. That's why this country is great."

"In future, better government will come to Nigeria," Elias said.

"I told you," Luke said, "that hope of my father's? It's why we're alive. It's what made us men."

"Well," Elias conceded. "There are graduates with masters' degrees in Nigeria who don't have jobs."

"Thousands and thousands of them," Susannah said.

"No jobs there for anyone," Abigail said.

"It's Nigeria," Luke said.

Then we were around the kitchen table, a pitcher of water at the center, each of us with a glassful. Elias asked Susannah, Samuel, Abigail, Marcus and Luke to sing an anthem now sung all over Ogoniland. It is said Ken Saro-Wiwa wrote the song in jail just before they killed him. The family looked at one another, a breath-held moment, and broke easily into four-part harmony, in fourths — that beautiful hollow-toned African sound.

> God who created Ogoniland,
> Beautiful land with blessings and honor,
> Give us joy and love and peace.
> Take away dishonesty and selfishness.
> Give us new life.
> Let our song rise above,
> Ogoni. Ogoni.
> Rise up. Arise.
> Take the glory and honor
> God gave to you with love.

As they sang, the family slipped back to a time before becoming Americans, each with his or her own determined and complex soul, back to a time when suffering was an act of love for God, their people, and their land, a time when they lived on hope, united with a cause, and their leader was alive.

As of 2023, Elias continued to travel between his Houston home and Nigeria.

And so soon we love this world, so soon we are willing to co-exist with dust in our eyes.

CLAUDIA RANKINE

I entered a fallow period of teaching, writing, and spending time with friends. During that period, Houston Grand Opera announced *The Refuge* to the board. There was a press release. The company performed a series of excerpts of the new work around Houston, at a Qawwali rock concert, a Russian meeting house, a Diwali festival, the Jewish Community Center. Ryan McKinney sang the anthem of South Vietnam in a ballroom atop Kim Son Restaurant.

I was working on the memoir the day Sue Elliott called and once again broke me out of that reverie. This call was a flat careful summons: Anthony Freud wanted to meet with me. I was in his office within the hour.

When I sat down with Freud that day, I was no longer someone newly returned to American society wondering how I would do what he was asking of me and why he was asking me. In a way, I had brought every one of my subjects there with me. One look at Freud's face full of concern, his lips drawn and tight, the crease in his forehead, and I told myself that even if *The Refuge* was cancelled, I would still have what I had gained. "Is there a problem?" I said.

Freud drew himself up, looking pragmatic, resigned. He had shared my libretto with the opera board, and it had not gone over well. The opera company's top dozen corporate donors were all oil or oil service companies, and most of the wealthiest of the board members worked in areas related to oil. I had done my Houston parlor game enough times — my version of six degrees of separation; scratch anyone in this city, and you get oil.

Freud leaned forward so that I could not avoid his eyes. There was sincerity and concern in his face. There had been a debate among the board, and a ruling. "In this production, you cannot say 'Ogoni,'" he said. "You cannot say 'oil,' and you certainly can't say 'Shell.'"

In that moment in his office, in my dismay, my bud of anger, I thought, *I should have known*. I should have known this could happen back when Elias first questioned my freedom to write; I should have known when I wrote parts of the Ogoni story into the libretto and doubts crept in that I pushed away; I should have known on the day that I picked up my head as I finished the work and then refused to acknowledge that exactly this could happen. I was no longer driven by starry-eyed faith in my new freedom, but as I finished that final draft, I had worked on myself to believe that in America, I really could live an unbounded sort of creative freedom. I wanted, no, *needed* to believe in art born of our fabled freedom of speech as my personal American Dream. I assured myself then that sponsors and leaders of the arts who supported my work would not allow this to happen, and that the opera company was not as dependent on corporate interests as the rest of us.

"Are you canceling the production?"

"No!" Freud said.

"Must I delete the African movement?"

"No," he said.

"Am I being censored?"

"No!" he said. "But we have this… problem."

The problem was one of message, of spin, so as not to risk millions of dollars in corporate donations that could just as well be directed elsewhere.

This was my introduction to hypervigilance in marketing that controls the message. I was new to this organizational self-censoring to finesse a pool of supporters, new to the enormity of the power of money over message, forces that were already beginning to take over our media and our world. To my fresh eyes, I saw fear in the organization. I thought it legitimate fear. Anthony looked as stricken as I felt.

I will admit here that even as a host of objections swelled inside of me, I was already working out how to comply with what he was asking of me. Some might say it was a sellout; others might call it adulthood, finally arrived. I thought of Binh a shoeless boy on the open sea, and Luisa walking the Texas desert, of crestfallen Ali confronting the FBI, Mythili and Murthy in love in a new way, lonely Manya finally free to cling to her religion, and all the others who had entrusted me with their stories and taught me so much. For their sakes, I would not say 'oil.' I would not say 'Ogoni,' and I would not say 'Shell,' not under their corporate umbrella. I would do what my subjects — my teachers — had done; I would follow the ways of this place where I had landed and find a way to thrive, and someday, I would tell the real story.

Once when I lived in the Hasidic world, mine were the only people fully real to me. I spent my days in swaths of cloth serving my husband and children as if we were the world. How certain, how grand we were. Now I had listened to people from around the globe and through them glimpsed who I might strive to be in this real, dirty, broken, amazing world.

Soon, I was back in Elias' family home. The family had gathered once again, and I had come to betray them. I dragged my heavy eyes up to meet those of forthright Elias whose God still led him, whose suffering people remained before him, for whom he continued to bear a degree of responsibility unfathomable in my soft life. I forced myself to meet Elias' eyes where I still found grave honesty. I forced myself to say, "I can't say 'Ogoni.' I can't say 'oil.' I can't say 'Shell.'" To Elias, Susannah, Samuel, Abigail, Marcus, and Luke, I said, "I misled you. I'm sorry."

There was dead silence.

Then, grace, bass-voiced Elias laughed, a genuine open-mouthed laugh, deep and felt and real. The family joined him. They exploded with it; guffaws, hoots, wry comments, pointing, holding their stomachs, wiping their eyes. I was stunned. "What is so funny?" I said.

"God!" Elias said. "God is funny! He saved us from certain death; then He made a miracle and brought us to the United States to give us new life, and deposited us in the city of, of... headquarters of Shell Oil!"

The family erupted. "Certainly, it's the funniest thing!" Abigail said.

"You knew?" I said. "You knew this would happen all along? You knew I wouldn't get to tell the Ogoni story?"

"You thought you could say those things in public!" Elias said. "Did you think we imagined for one minute that Shell Oil would allow you to do that?"

Unlike me, for Elias and his family, American freedom had never been such a blinding light in their eyes that they failed to see how our freedom might be qualified. They knew all too well how inexorable the corporate steamroller was over lives and governments. Elias had seen my ignorance and knew their story would probably be stopped. He and the family had still chosen to tell it. Maybe they did so simply because, in America, they still could.

"Thank you for your invitation to your show," Elias said. "We will not be attending."

In the car outside of their home, I had a long and useless cry.

The Refuge debuted on November 8th, 2007, on the main stage of Houston's Wortham Center — an imposing and elegant opera house that stands a block from the seat of city government. After appearing in a series of televised announcements about this event, Mayor Bill White came out on stage opening night to introduce the work. *Naxos* Recording was there, and a New York Times reviewer was in the audience. I disappeared with Chris to a box seat high above.

That night as the stories unfolded in song, I became Binh once again, and I became Luisa, Mythili, Murthy, Ali, and Manya. I became the Ogoni people, and every one of the others who had shared their lives with me. I was of a people of my own now, too, and understood better what that meant, who we were and what my family had lost. In a way, I had become my eclectic country, land of the free, magnet for the masses, the same that napalmed Vietnamese villages and funneled dark money to Salvadoran murder squads, that kidnapped thousands of children at the border, and continually sucked oil from Nigeria like blood from a tit, the same that daily toggled between professing freedom for its people and corporate greed, yet remained a beacon of hope and home for so many, where I could live well and speak freely.

Well then, I thought, if I was my country, I must have a similar potential for evil coupled with inclination to good. It means I have the same tendency to believe our myths even when they're exposed as myths, and the same desire to open my arms to people flung from their homes around the world, to appease my American guilt, yes, and also because of my humanity. Sitting next to Chris in the dark that night, his music, our work, flowed out of all of this. Then, someone dressed in black appeared at our side like a shadow with a murmur and a pin light to lead us through a back passage and up inner stairs to the stage.

Before all that, before the premiere began, I stood in the velvet carpeted atrium watching the glittering crowd arrive, scattered among them people in an array of colorful costumes from around the world. Despite his refusal to attend, I looked a long time for tall, stately Elias. He'd make a grand arrival in striking African robes surrounded by his family. I wanted to tell Elias what he already knew, that like the Ogoni who speak many dialects and languages, in this country, too, it really is only about the people in all our variety and our dependence on the health of the land.

I wanted to tell Elias that I had learned from him in what way my freedom is limited and fragile. I wanted to tell him that, like him and his family, I will continue to speak, because in America, I still can.

Intermezzo

Voices

From Nigeria:
"My grandfather was an Oba. He was crowned by the British. We had servants; I was a soft boy, so how was I to know what to do with a gun?

"They forced me into the army at seventeen. I don't want to tell you the horrors I saw. It wasn't an army. I fought only to survive, killing if that's what it took, eating what I had to, seeing what no one should see. When it was over, I was a man. I swore I'd leave and never go back."

From Liberia:
"I followed my brother to Houston because of the Nike t-shirts and tennis shoes he sent me... and the chance to get an education so I could feed my family back home. I felt so free here, everything so clean, but I always thought I would go home again. That was before my brother went back; before they came at night and took my father for questioning; before my brother dared to go ask where our father was and they killed him, too; before my brother

Anthony joined a group and escaped the rebels. He walked a hundred miles, eating leaves, sick, stumbling in the heat and dust, past swollen bodies on the ground, while I watched the revolution on CNN in my t-shirt and tennis shoes.

"It was two years before I knew who was alive and who was dead."

From El Salvador:
"I remember the cooling feel of bare feet on ceramic tiles, and the view of the volcano from our window. There was a wall around our home for safety. Inside it, we had trees of guava, mango, maranon — we had fruit with every meal. I remember rain, rain so many days, and lightning at night that mixed with the sound of the bombs so that I didn't know which it was that cut off our electricity again. Then, there was my father in the doorway saying his plane crashed while he was crop dusting, but he had to be joking because here he was, alive. He said someone cut his fuel lines. I remember hearing shouts from my bed at night from the demonstrations in the neighborhood, and the taste of ice on a stick made of rice and cinnamon or frozen fruit juice with chunks of fruit. I remember my school in an old convent, the silence, and the cobbled courtyards. Each courtyard had a dripping fountain.

"There was the ringing in the dark. It was the telephone. A man was calling to warn us he'd been hired to kill my father. In no time, we were gone."

From Democratic Republic of Congo:
"When you grow up in a dictatorship, you breathe fear; you always know you can be killed. Then, when you meet new ideas for the first time, it's a thrill. It all seems so true. You feel, you know, that a deep relief is coming.

"They told us the story of Jesus. They said it was okay that he died, that he was here to make a difference. They made me feel that, even if they killed me, at least I could make a difference.

"Then, police found our meeting and arrested us. They tortured me every day for two months. Despair brought me back to myself. I remembered my mother, and my sisters. I didn't want to die.

"They released me like a rabbit they wanted to follow back to its hole. I didn't go home. I got out of the country alive.

"I work in IT for the City of Houston. When you've been tortured, your mind doesn't let you go back home."

From Democratic Republic of Congo (phone conversation):
"I am my sister's son. She didn't give birth to me! She married an American missionary, and they

adopted me after they moved here. How else was I going to get a green card?

"My mother had birthed me by herself in her field in eastern Congo, and she cut the cord herself, and me, fourteen years old, on an adventure in small town Kansas. I had thought the whole world was Black!

"I knew so little English I couldn't tell what was prejudice and what was simple dislike because the people there thought me stupid. As a schoolchild in Lukweyi, I was often honored to raise the flag in the schoolyard because of my grades. I made speeches.

"After I got married in Houston, we brought my father here. He was eighty-four. He had lived all his life in Bandundu, mostly outdoors. He said if we didn't send him back home, he would hurt himself, and it would be a curse on the family. He said he could not stay alone all day indoors and watch me use precious water on the lawn.

"I'm a microbiologist. I work at MD Anderson. Wait a minute while I pick up my daughter from daycare. Hi baby, you want pizza? Daddy's here."

From Nigeria:
"It's been twenty-four years but there's this pull on my heart that says, *You need to go back home.* Everyone there is my brother, my sister. We are one open, exposed nerve. We hurt, we cry, we laugh,

we celebrate, and we do it all in the open — a shared experience. We don't know how to keep things in.

"We had this cul-de-sac of buildings, and at night everyone sat outside like a family. You never knew whose home was whose. If you didn't have a television, you went in to someone else's to watch."

From Gujarat, India (wife died just before he emigrated to the US with his children):
"I never cried. I will not marry again; I will be strong for my children, but when I am old, I will go home to my friends. I will come back here and visit every year, spend two, three months seeing my children, this one, then that one, and the rest of the year I will stay home. I wish for that."

From Chechnya:
"The Caucasus Mountains were always green, and everyone in the village was my cousin."

From Democratic Republic of Congo:
If someone was going away to university, everyone gave him something — money, food, gifts. Then, when he came home with a college degree, the whole village celebrated for days."

From El Salvador:

"My brother got accepted to college after we'd been in the United States for two years. We packed up and moved there with him.

"That's my family! We stay together. We never understood the American teen who says, 'Hey! Could you drop me off at the corner?'"

From Democratic Republic of Congo:

"One day, I drove a friend to Memorial for her work. I saw so many trees! I asked my friend, 'Why do these rich people live in the bush?' She laughed and said, 'With what they spend on one tree, you could buy a house!' So, why did people tell me I came from the jungle?

"Around my father's house were beautiful trees. They were mango, and rubber. We planted them for ventilation."

From El Salvador:

"Sometimes, I walk into my Houston home, and I say, 'Yes! There's electricity!'"

From Cuba (we named The Refuge after this quote):

"There was this building in Miami where they gave us English lessons, job training, and peanut butter. We called that place, 'El Refugio.'"

From Mexico:

"August the second, I got my citizenship at the federal building. That day was the best day of my life, because when they told me to say the Pledge of Allegiance to the flag, in my heart was that I was here and at the same time in Mexico, but also that I want this, and that I will be a good citizen of the United States of America.

"In this moment, I remembered all of my childhood, and how I always wanted this. Now whenever I see the US flag I think, *This flag is a symbol of all of my story.*

Coda:
Meditation on Freedom

Roberto, *Cuba*

"Why did I leave my country and so many not? How was I different? The reason I come to the United States is because I don't want to be slave. I want to be free man. This is true: everyone in Cuba is slave, but I am me, myself, my person. Over there, they don't let me belong to myself. My life don't belong to me.

"What is slave? A slave is a person who don't own his time, not for himself and not for his family. In Cuba, you belong to government. I tried twenty years to stay, but how can I tell you? You have only one life, and you don't want to miss the chance to have that life.

Over there, you don't ever say what you have inside of you, and what is outside of you is not you. You cannot do anything that is who you are. You don't *have* opinions. This is living a nightmare.

"Every day in Cuba, I get up from the bed, and I don't say one word. I look in the mirror and know I am a man who don't have a tomorrow because tomorrow I will do exact same like today. In Cuba, you must do same every day — live how government say you must be living. Can't change nothing. No hoping. No future. You are not working for economic reasons; you live for government. Many people under communism, they don't realize, but for people who are thinking, they see the walls.

"Modern slave is worse than Roman slave because when you are modern slave, you are slave who can read books and see authors have opinions. You know soul and freedom. How hard it is to be slave who can read and write and recognize what he don't have.

"It's the walls.

"The communists, they are putting fear inside you. For many, better not to think.

"I know why people don't leave Cuba because I lived it. Most people in Cuba, they go, go like lambs. I know that nature; I know how people stay afraid inside themselves. You lose yourself. You can't think to try to leave because, if you think, you cannot bear it, but you know inside yourself that every day you stay, you are someone who surrenders. You look in the mirror, and you know you are communist collaborator selling your soul. Then you wake up next day and surrender again. When you have children, you don't want to surrender them, too.

"Now, I can laugh. Only now.

"This is why me and my wife, we make a raft. We were ready to leave any way we can and cross the Florida straits. I was not coming to the United States because I want the United States, but because I want to leave the nightmare I have every day in Cuba. I did not know what is here. Lucky for us, we come to best place for freedom.

"The great of this country is, they allow you to be part of working for solutions. Life here is working with a purpose toward solution of problems. If you have the problems but you can't be part of the solution, better to die.

"Oh man, how can I tell you how great, how good I feel in the United States? I did not expect to find society with this organization, this respect for law, this recognizing order. How fair the social system here. *This* is land of milk and honey, not Jerusalem — America. I never found people more loving, more taking care of each other. How they cheer and respect one for the other. Don't matter what social position, what race. I am satisfied with my sacrifice for twenty years to come to know this. If it comes that I must do it again, I would do it again."

Acknowledgements

With gratitude to my wife Susan, my love and my anchor. To Rich Levy and Marilyn Jones, twin sparks who started all of this by giving Houston Grand Opera exactly one name for their project. To Christopher Theofanidis, who listened between the lines and made magic with his music. A deep bow to Anthony Freud, Perryn Leech, Sue Elliott, conductor Patrick Summers, and everyone else at the opera company who brought *The Refuge* into being. To singers Jamie Barton, Ryan McKinny, Liam Bonner, Faith Sherman, Beau Gibson, Albina Shagimuratova, and Rebekah Camm who went on to world-class singing careers. To family and friends too many to name who listened, mentored me through my neuroses, read bad versions, and provided a shoulder, patient feedback, writing space, needed distractions, coffee, friendship, and unearned applause; Debbie Angel, Rich Levy, Cami Ostman, Katy Miner, Rosellen Brown, Robin Greene, Stefani Twyford, and Lori Laitman — you are my standouts. Above all, to the one hundred twenty-three people who mustered the fortitude to leave their homes and come to the United States, and then had the courage to re-live, into a microphone, events that in most cases they didn't want to have gone through even once, from the bottom of my heart, thank you.

Libretto

The Refuge

AFRICA
chorus, children's chorus, soli, and orchestra

<u>Ensemble</u>:
[*clapping*]

<u>Tenor</u>:
My dad was always preaching:

<u>Chorus</u>:
'Better days are coming.'

<u>Tenor</u>:
My dad was always preaching:

<u>Chorus</u>:
'Better days are coming.'

<u>Tenor</u>:
'Trust me now.
We will have good times again.'

Chorus:
Better days
Oh, better days.

Tenor:
We will have good times again.

Chorus:
Better days are coming.

Tenor:
You hear that every day,
it becomes your backbone.

Chorus:
Dad was a leader.

[*Orchestra*]

Soprano:
We begged him.
We begged him to leave.
We begged our father to go,
but he wouldn't.

Chorus:
They came…
Then they came…

Soprano:
They tore up our land.
They tore up the streets where we walked,
where we lived.

Chorus:
Soldiers came and took him from our house.

Entire Ensemble:
Smoke and fire out of the ground.
Nothing grows.

Mezzo-soprano:
They torched all of our land.

Chorus:
Nothing grows.

Quartet: *soprano, mezzo, tenor, baritone*
Bodies in dirt, bodies in streams.
Nothing grows.
Death in the water,
death in the air.
Nothing grows.
Dying so common,
you stop caring.

Chorus:
Fish die. People die.
Then you die,
like something without value.

Men of the Chorus:
Running, running, through the bush.
Running, running, through the grass.
Day and night, night and day, and night.

Baritone:
My grandfather was an Oba,
crowned by the British.
We had servants — I was a soft boy,
so how was I to know
what to do with a gun?
They forced me into the army
at seventeen. It wasn't an army.
I fought only to survive, killing,
if that's what it took, eating
what I had to, seeing
what no one should see.
When it was over, I was a man.
I swore I'd leave and never go back.

Women of the Chorus:
When you're pregnant, you can't be happy.
How to keep my children alive?
The only thing is to hope in God.

<u>Chorus</u>:
Running, running through the bush.
Running through the grass.

<u>Men of the Chorus</u>:
Got to get away.

<u>Chorus</u>:
Day and night, night and day.
I don't know. I can't tell.
I want water. I want my mother.

<u>Baritone</u>:
I have to get away. Have to get away…

<u>Chorus</u>:
[*Repeats*]
They come,

<u>Trio</u>: *soprano, mezzo-soprano, tenor*
When people hear an army truck, they run
and yell, and you run, too.
You don't ask questions.

<u>Soprano</u>:
They came into the house.
They lifted their *kobokos*
and beat me, kick me.

Men:
Where is your husband? Where is he?
He preaches against our government!

Mezzo-soprano:
'No!' I say, 'No!'
They beat me.
Beat me… [*Fading*]

Chorus:
[*Repeats*]
One of them said to kill me.
The other one said, 'No.'

Soprano:
Where are my brothers
and my sisters?
I have to keep them close.
Where are my brothers?
I have to keep them close.
Where are my sisters?
I have to keep them close.

Mezzo-soprano:
Day is night, night is day.
Running, running through the bush,

<u>Chorus</u>:
Where is your father? Where is he?
Where is your brother? Where is he?
Where is your sister? Where is she?
Where is your mother? Where?
Where is she? Where?

<u>Chorus and soloists</u>:
One said kill me.
One said kill me.
One said kill me.
One said kill me.
I want my mother.

It's Dad! Our father!
They've killed him!
Dad! Our leader!
Killed him! They've killed him!

[*Orchestra: new and hopeful tone.*]

<u>Chorus, Soprano, Mezzo-soprano</u>:
Don't cry. Be still.

[*Orchestra*]

<u>Duet</u>: *tenor, soprano*
There are beds in America — feels strange,
and enough food for everyone, like it's nothing.

<u>Children's Chorus</u>:
I get to go to school.
I
Want to be a teacher.
But I have to sit
in a desk
and wear shoes.
At first, I used to run away,
but then, I didn't.

<u>Baritone</u>:
I went to Sharpstown High, and kids said:
'You are not from here.'

<u>Baritone and Children's Chorus</u>:
Are you from Africa? You a monkey?
And what's a refugee, anyway?

<u>Baritone</u>:
Feels strange.

<u>Duet</u>: *mezzo-soprano, soprano*
Feels strange.
Will it ever feel like home in America?
If I'm here, how can I help my people?

<u>Children's Chorus</u>:
In school, I like to work.

I like to go to school.
I want to be a teacher.

Tenor:
I can run for Congress.

Baritone:
I can work.

Mezzo-soprano:
I can go to church.

Duet: *soprano, mezzo-soprano*
We brought my father to Houston from Africa,
He said he couldn't sit alone all day indoors
and watch us use precious water
For the lawn.

Baritone:
Six dollars an hour, twenty hours a day,
And when I could buy an old car,
I fell asleep at the wheel and totaled it.
At least I could sleep on buses,
And there was no fear in the night.
No more hiding
because I dared to denounce them.
No more desperate eyes. No more desperate lies.
No more dead lying on the ground untended.
And every night, I go to sleep

with my family around me.
And wake up in the morning.
I just wish…

Chorus:
I wish my people would be safe in Nigeria.

Children's Chorus:
[*Shouted*]
No, we don't miss Africa!
Just, all the time
we want to sing our songs
from home!

Entire Ensemble:
Mboka Nzambe eza mabe,
kati na biso bana ya Afrika
Tolingana tosangana
libota moko.

*The land of God has gone astray within us children
of Africa. Let's love each other and unite as one.*

VIETNAM

tenor, mezzo-soprano, baritone, dan bau, and orchestra

Tenor:
A gram of gold — my mother's gift.
That's what I have from her.

Tenor:
I stand on the bridge outside of town
laughing with friends in the moonlight.
A small boat begins to move away.
My friends dare me, and I dive.
I jump the boat for fun, for a short ride,
but then we move into open sea.
A man comes out to say:
'We're not going back, or they will kill me.'
I was thirteen. I had no shoes.

I never saw
my mother again.

I remember the sound at the fence
at the refugee camp.
People yelling names.
They called me 'orphan.'
Me — orphan.
My brothers scattered from Vietnam
like marbles tossed across a map.

We sat in refugee camps in three countries
until the Red Cross put us together again.

We were sent to my uncle in Houston.
I went to Aldine High. I worked three jobs —
it was magic to earn money.
I bought a car. Someday,
I would drive my mother
home.

She died alone in Vietnam
while I was studying to be a doctor.
My neighbor — my mother's friend — sent a letter.
    At her funeral, five white headbands,
the mourner's sign, lay across her bed
because her children were not there
to wear them.
The neighbor sent this single gram of gold
worth twelve dollars
my mother had saved
for my wedding.

[*Orchestra*]

Baritone:
I was a soldier for the South Vietnamese.
When the North won the war,
I was arrested.

Mezzo-soprano:
I wait for him in Saigon,
but, no money, and communists, very bad.
No hope for our ten children.
We got away in my boat.
I left everything: I left him.
Just me and the children. Very bad.

Baritone:
They took us north to a prison camp.
I worked rice fields many years,
always silent.

Mezzo-soprano:
Will he remember me?

Mezzo-soprano:
Houston.
Fifteen years I don't see him.
Every day, only work.
Store, home, home, store.

Baritone:
Hot sun, steaming.
Always bent over.

Mezzo-soprano:
The children come to me after school.
Oldest daughter cooks at home.

Store, home, home, store.
Will he come back to me?

Baritone:
Does she know I'm alive?

Mezzo-soprano:
Come back to me!

Baritone:
Does she know I'm alive?
I smuggled letters out to her.
Did she get them?
I tried to escape,
and one day, I succeeded.

I walked across the whole country.
I walked across Vietnam.
I walked across the dangerous roads.
Come back to her.

Duet: *baritone and mezzo-soprano*
Came back to me/came back to her
Fifteen years of working, hoping,
Fifteen years of working, waiting.
He/she remembered me.

Baritone:
My children remembered me.

But everything here is strange
and people say,
'You are not from here.'
I sit in store and study English from books.
It's very hard to be an immigrant —
every day, only work, and all the time,
so much nostalgia.

Mezzo-soprano:
The children made good lives here.
All married and finished their education.

Duet: *baritone and mezzo-soprano*
They are from here.
But so many memories…

Baritone:
[*Spoken*]
I still think of Vietnam — all those years working
rice fields, always silent. Late nights in the dark
barracks while the guards were asleep, we used
to sing forbidden songs…

[*South Vietnamese national anthem, a nineteenth
century military march, here sung as an elegy.*]

Này Công Dân ơi! Quc gia đ n ngày gii phóng
Đng lòng cùng đi hy sinh ti c gì thân sng.
Vì tương lai Quc Dân, cùng xông pha khói tên,

Làm sao cho núi sông t nay luôn vng b n.
Dù cho phơi thây trên gươm giáo,
Thù nưc, ly máu đào đem báo.
Nòi ging lúc bi n phi cn gii nguy,
Ngưi Công Dân luôn vng b n tâm trí.
Hùng tráng quy t chi n đu làm cho khp nơi
Vang ti ng ngưi nưc Nam cho đ n muôn đi!
Công Dân ơi! Mau hi n thân dưi c!
Công Dân ơi! Mau làm cho cõi b
Thoát cơn tàn phá, v vang nòi ging
Xng danh nghìn năm giòng ging Lc Hng!

MEXICO
chorus, soprano, orchestra

Mexican Woman:
[*Spoken*]
Parts of my family have been here one hundred and
    fifty years, because when they came, they
    didn't leave Mexico — Texas was part of us.
    In a way, we are still Mexicans.

Men of the Chorus:
We were six the first time Daddy took us
to pick tomatoes, peppers, corn.
We rode to market on the truck bed.
He got twenty-five pesos for one day, we got half.

I think we may be finished
school to the fourth grade.
Our village was all women and children.
All men went Norte — Daddy, too.

The first time we cross the Rio,
we swim, we hide,
we get past the *migras*,
found our daddy.
He was so proud.

Chorus:
You have to know how to get in the river,
know the water, know when to swim.
You have to know how to get in the river.
Let it carry you! It's all right —
the Rio will carry you
to the other side.

The World Cup was playing in Mexico City
and everyone there was going nuts,
but nobody here gives a damn about soccer!
That was the first shock.

Women:
We moved in with our aunt,
five of us in one bedroom,
and in the other room,
a married couple, their two kids,

and a woman who walked here from Mexico
in high heels.

Chorus:
Older siblings dropped out of school,
dropped out to help: mechanic's assistant,
cook, baker, KMart cashier.
But at least here,
the bathrooms were indoors.

You got to get into the Rio.
Get into the Rio, don't be afraid.
You got to get into the Rio —
let it carry you!

In the laundromat across the street,
we put in pesos
instead of quarters
and it worked!

Working for my kids to get
graduated from the school.
It's all for them.

Women:
We rode the bus at night,
in the cold, rain, and hot. So hot.
Waiting so long to get on and go,
and on the bus, angry faces

Some of them say:
'You are not from here.'

No room for you, sorry… [*Repeats*]

But all the time, our mother says:
'God takes care of us.
We must be grateful.'

Men of the Chorus:
The good thing
about speaking another language
is that you can pretend
you don't understand.

Women of the Chorus:
Mom learned English watching Mister Rogers.
He talked so slow and clear.
She cried when he died.
She cried.

Men of the Chorus:
You know how one friend
might welcome you
and bring you a drink,
but the other is a better friend
because he lets you go to the refrigerator yourself?
Houston is that kind of friend.

Even with no papers, we still say:
'This is our country now.'
We like the way that here,
you don't need to pay the police.
There are pretty fair laws.
We just wish we could be
legal.

Chorus:
Working for my kids to get
graduated from the school.
It's all for them.

Women of the Chorus:
I took my kids to the park
(they are not so dark like me)
and someone heard me speaking Spanish to them.
She said, 'How much do you charge to babysit?
I want to know: can you be my maid?'

Chorus:
Working for my kids to get
graduated from the school.
It's all for them. All for them

Soprano:
I was fourteen when Mom left.
I stayed in Mexico with my sister.
Mom sent money every week.

When she called, we said:
'Everything is fine.'
She trusted her family
to take care of us.
Nobody take care of us.
Her cousin raped me.
I never told.

Sometimes I think it's better
To stay behind with your kids
And fight together to live.
You're not gonna take away pain
with money.

Chorus:
During the ceremony in the federal building
to get our citizenship,
we remembered our childhood,
and how we wished to come here.
And we were thinking,
Now, I am from here.

You got to get into the Rio,
And let it bring you.
Don't be afraid.
You got to get into the Rio,
Let it carry you.

PAKISTAN-INDIA
Part One: Pakistan
*mezzo, soprano, tenor, baritone, orchestra,
harmonium*

Pakistani woman:
[*Spoken*]
People speak to me in Spanish. They think I'm
Latino! I say I don't understand. They say, 'Shame
on you! Your parents didn't teach you your own
language?' I say, 'But I'm from Pakistan!'
You know? The British gave us a complex about
our own language. Spanish-speaking people have
lived here four hundred years and they still love
their language! I learned something from that. They
are why I only speak Urdu to my baby.

[Qawaali singer improvises on *Yeh Jo Halka
Halka*, with harmonium.]

Mezzo-soprano:
I still remember the thick stone walls
cool to the touch, the hot nights I slept
on the marble floor. The colors of the flowers
in our garden, the smell of Karachi
in the summer air, mixed with the sound
of Muslim prayer.

<u>Soprano</u>:
All that family left behind.
There were thirty in our home —
every weekend a feast.
The smells, the spices.
Oh, I remember!
My sisters, my best friends.
The secrets we shared,
all of us so close and noisy.

<u>Tenor and Baritone</u>:
Just like home.

<u>Tenor</u>:
I was a dreamer, and in Pakistan,
that's like committing a crime.
I was a visionary, and in Pakistan,
that's like committing a crime.

<u>Tenor and Baritone</u>:
Just like home...

<u>Baritone</u>:
We were eight children in one house
when my brother left for America.
He sent me a postcard of a red convertible.
That was it: I followed him.
Of course, I followed him.

Tenor and Baritone:
Just like home…

Soprano:
My husband left for America.
Of course, I followed him.
We chose Houston because of the weather.
I loved it here. At first,
I would go outside
just to smell the air.
Just like Karachi.

Trio: *soprano, tenor, baritone*
Just like home…

Mezzo-soprano:
At first, I never went outside.
I always locked the doors.
I called my mother in Pakistan,
'Come get me. Come get me!'
I turned on music from home
because I felt alone.

Quartet: *soprano, mezzo-soprano, tenor, baritone*
There are no mountains here,
and no old buildings.
Everything
too new, too clean.

<u>Quartet</u>: *soprano, mezzo-soprano, tenor, baritone*
Feels like home…

<u>Baritone</u>:
I went to school and couldn't speak.
So shy, and soft,
like a tomato.
There was one Filipino boy —
we played basketball.
He's still my best friend.

<u>Mezzo-soprano</u>:
In Pakistan, you had no choice about religion.
There was a mosque on every corner,
strict rules about the faith,
and you believed. Oh, you believed.

I still pray, and read my holy Koran,
but I'm confused to talk to my daughters
about religion. I teach them, don't lie,
respect people, do good stuff,
but they play tennis and swim.
How can I say, don't wear shorts,
cover your head?
We're not the same anymore.

<u>Quartet</u>: *soprano, mezzo-soprano, tenor, baritone*
[*Wailing tone*]
Ah…

Baritone:
I had a suitcase of dirty clothes and some music.
Nothing more. I worked hard, but then I found her
    She had blonde hair,
from Oklahoma,
and I loved her. Oh, I loved her.
My family would never understand.
I was a good husband, always working.
The culture where you grow up
makes you assume things that aren't spoken,
just understood. When she left me,
neither of us could explain why.

Tenor:
Since Nine Eleven,
I've been interrogated six times by the FBI
because I was against the war.
That broke my heart.
Until then I felt
this was my home.
I told each one of those interrogators:
'Where I come from,
I didn't have the freedom
to say what I believe.
I'm not letting you take that away from me here.
This is my home now.'

Quartet: *soprano, mezzo-soprano, tenor, baritone*

If a time comes that we have to leave,
we will know how to do that.

Baritone:
I will know how to do that.

Quartet: *soprano, mezzo-soprano, tenor, baritone*
But for our children, we want their heart and soul
    to be right here in the USA,
to never go through what we went through,
to believe they can be anything they want to be.

Chorus:
Feels like home...

PAKISTAN-INDIA
Part Two: India
soprano, mezzo-soprano, baritone, two sitars,
tabla, and orchestra

Soprano:
My mother played *sarasvati veena*,
named for the goddess of knowledge.
Its strings over wood and gold.
She sat, arms like a caress,
and laid one side so gently on her lap.
She sang with it like a lover.

Indian music filled me;
Made me understand human beings;
Made me understand myself.
Her voice was high, rich, godly.

Mezzo-soprano and baritone:
I used to tell my parents, 'Not me!
I'm going to have a love marriage!'

Mezzo-soprano:
But I'm Indian…

Baritone:
You accept what life brings.
My parents had already chosen her.
She was a good Brahmin girl.

Mezzo-soprano:
Felt odd, sitting with a strange man.

Baritone:
Felt odd, sitting with a strange girl.

Baritone and Mezzo-soprano:
Here to marry me.
Thousands came to the wedding.
The family was in debt for years!
We escaped right away to the States.
What a shock!

<u>Baritone</u>:
She didn't know how to cook.

<u>Mezzo-soprano</u>:
He didn't know how to drive.

<u>Baritone</u>:
She didn't know how to clean.

<u>Duet</u>: *baritone and mezzo-soprano*
We only knew about milk from cows,
Not cartons.
We are vegetarians.

<u>Baritone</u>:
I got used to pizza. I got used to it.
Actually — if I can be honest with you,
I love pizza.

<u>Baritone</u>:
She made her grandmother's lentil soup
with tomatoes. I survived.

<u>Mezzo-soprano</u>:
He never complains.

<u>Baritone</u>:
I survived.

She didn't know how to cook.

Mezzo-Soprano:
He never complains.

Baritone:
She didn't know how to clean.

Mezzo-Soprano:
He never complains.

Baritone:
I got used to pizza.

Mezzo-soprano and Baritone:
We only knew about milk from cows.

Baritone:
In India, we were surrounded by family.
Here, there was no one else.

Duet: *mezzo-soprano, baritone*
We became partners here.
Our life together began here.
Our home is our little world.

[*Reflective*]
Mezzo-soprano:
Some days I feel I belong here.

Baritone:
…and some days, I feel I don't belong anywhere,
but I know this: because I am here,
I'm somehow more Indian than before.

Soprano:
In India, you open the door, step out,
and suddenly,
you are surrounded with
so many colors and smells.
Remembering home makes life here seem…

I don't believe in religion per se,
But I always remember.
That's why I keep the Hindu festivals,
Prepare the foods
and teach my daughter Shuvha
how the gods and goddesses
are just different faces
Of one great God.

JEWS FROM THE FORMER USSR
various soli, orchestra

Mezzo-Soprano II:
[*From a dark stage*]
He beat me. He tried to rape me.

He screamed, 'You Jew!
You are all Russians' problems!'

Mezzo-Soprano I:
He held my friend backwards over a hot stove.
'You Jew!' he said. He was tall.
I pulled his jacket.
The others looked and said
nothing.

Baritone:
In a way, we were not Jews in Russia.
Our Jewish traditions were banned.
Tradition has to come from childhood
or you don't feel the need,
and religion comes from tradition.
They stole that from us, too.

Tenor:
So how did I know I was Jewish?
It was written on my ID card!

Ensemble (all six soloists):
Party positions, most universities, many jobs,
closed to the Jews. Only a few openings
in science or medicine
for the lucky ones.
Cruel, people are cruel.
They still loved Stalin

who killed so many Jews.

Mezzo-Soprano II:
They said in school there is no God.
But even as a girl, I said, 'It could be
that there is a God.'
'If there was a God,' they said,
'Prayers would get answered.'
Go ahead!' they told us. 'Pray for candy!'
'If there was a God,' they said,
'He wouldn't allow cosmonauts
to go into heaven.
A powerful ruler like this God
does not allow invaders into his territory.'
But I always thought,
Maybe there is a God.

Soprano:
Passover, we carried the matzoh
from my grandmother's house at night,
hidden, although we didn't know
how to make a seder.
My father sent us outside
to look for informers
before he told us
about his Jewish childhood.
Only then we ate.

Ensemble:

To apply to emigrate
was seven hundred dollars —
at least eight month's pay
to escape from Russia.
Cruel, people are cruel.
You can't sell your belongings.
You must leave your job
even if it will take years to get an answer,
and you may never return.

Baritone:
So many people who applied to emigrate,
instead of going to the US or Israel
as they had dreamed, were sent to Siberia.

Tenor:
After I left, I asked a HIAS man
in the Red Cross Camp:
'Please, may I *not* go to Israel?'
He looked at me, and said,
'You can go anywhere you want.
You are in a free place now.'
I didn't know what it means
to be free. Even now,
when I tell this, I cry.

Ensemble:
And then we came.

Soprano:
[*Spoken*]

We fill out many papers. Then I read, 'sex.' I ask the man, 'You want to know about that, too?'

Tenor:
[*Spoken*]
The social worker offered me 'sofa.' I said, 'Sofa' is name for Russian woman. Why I want Sofa if I have my wife?'

Mezzo-Soprano I:
[*Spoken*]
I got a job in a Houston clothing store. A customer came and he said, 'Where are your bras?' I think fast. Bra, bra… means lamp in Russian, but this is English. I ask him, 'You want this for man or for woman?'

Trio:
I have college education
but I come here to America
and feel like child.
I have college education but
cannot express myself
for simple things.
Cannot express myself.

[orchestra]

Baritone:
I came to a decision because I am here now,
free to think and believe:
I believe in God. I am scientist; this is logic.
I believe in a creator of cosmic order
who gave us soul.

Baritone:
At forty-seven, I had a Bar Mitzvah.
I spoke from the pulpit
about my right to be a Jew.
I didn't do it
to be a religious person.
We were not allowed, and we lost that.
I did it to show those Soviet bastards
that now I can be who I am.
I am here now. I am from here.
And I am a Jew.

[Ends with decisive chords from bayan.]

CENTRAL AMERICA
soprano, orchestra

<u>Soprano</u>:
We lived in San Salvador.
There was a gang that knew
we had cash in the house.
They only wanted to rob us.
They even knocked first.

It was my mother -
She tried to close the door
when she saw they had guns.
I heard the shot.
My mother… all of her blood.
What's happening?

And the last man
Ran away.

One of them came back.
'*You saw, you saw.*'
'No, no,' I say. 'No.'
'*You saw.*
And if you talk,
we will kill you'.

Walking, hiding, hiding, walking,
always afraid.

I went away to another city
But… they found me.
They always find you.

'*You will talk.*'
'No!' I say.
'Yes, you will,
and when you do,
we will kill you.'
'No, please, no.
I won't say
anything.'

Every week a letter came:
If she talks, we will kill her.
Finally, I was brave enough
to go out to the store.

They caught me.
They raped me.
They beat me.
They are the ones:
the fathers
of my son.

Walking, hiding
Always afraid.
Santa Rosa de Lima —
another city, another start.

Just me and my
toddling boy.

My new husband —
he cared for me.
I cared for him.
When he left for America,
he said he'd send money.
And soon,
we would follow.
He promised.
I trusted him.
Until he found an Americana on the other side
and left us hungry.

More letters came to my brother.
'She will talk.'
And soon.
'She will talk.'
They will find me.
Brother, keep him safe.
Protect him.
I will go to Estados Unidos
And send for him.
My boy, I don't want you to look
When I leave.

In Chiapas, I asked an old man about a bus.
He said, 'You are not from here.

Aren't you afraid?'
If they arrest me, I will come again.
I'll beg if I have to,
I will make it
to Estados Unidos.

Walking, hiding
Riding, waiting.
Walking, running.

'Papers, papers!' the officer shouted.
I shook so much he knew.
'Are you from here?
Get off the bus.
Why are you crying?'

'They killed my mother.
I left my child.
You will send me back
to start again.'

He put fifty Mexican pesos in my hand.
I got back on the bus.

Walking, hiding,
so many days and nights.
Crackers and water and
cactus thorns.
My shoes can't close.

My feet are bleeding.
I'm alone with six men.
I keep myself apart… and pray.

I hear the truck horn.
I am afraid.
I have to get over the wall.
The six men
tear shirts, tear skin;
they pull me over the wall
into the truck.
They save me.

For eight hours,
we lay on top of each other
like pieces of wood.
When we stopped,
we were afraid to breathe.

I called my husband:
'Do you have the courage
To tell that Americana
It's your *wife* on the 'phone?'

But I forgave him.
He came back to me.
I didn't have anyone else.
Just him.

The coyote promised
the boy will be safe.
But he's so small.
The coyote promised
they'll only put him in the trunk
for the crossing.

But he put him
Beneath an eighteen-wheeler.
The noise, the vibration —
Hold on, my boy, hold on!
Don't die.

At the border
the coyote betrayed me.
He gave my son
To Immigration.

Not one friend or relative
would go for him.
I gave myself up
to claim him.

And when I came, the officer said:
'You are not from here.
Aren't you afraid?'

The lawyers say
I don't have a case.

Where can I go now?
All I have is this order for deportation.

Soon, I'll be walking, walking,
so many days and nights.
Crackers and water and cactus thorns,
I know I can do this.
I know I can, because
I know how.

FINALE
ensemble and orchestra

Walking, walking day and night,
Walking and running day and night.
A gram of gold, a fistful of earth,
that's what I have from home.
Driving, hoping, running, hiding,
hoping to be free. Running, hiding to be free.

Walking and running day and night.
All our hope is here.
Now, we are you.
Our struggles are your struggles.
I am from here.